MY TESTIMONY

MARY BOOTH

Come to the Fire

FOREWORD

I first met Mary Warburton Booth, in the autumn of 1913, when she came to Ludhiana to conduct the opening meetings for our Medical Students.

She had then been in India about five years. The following spring we traveled home together for furlough, and spent an unforgettable time in Palestine, following the footsteps of our Master and reading His Word in the different places where He had lived and taught.

What remains most vividly in my memory of her, is that she was such a personal friend of the Lord, working not only for Him, but with Him. There was the solemn hush of His presence and His power. She was quick to recognize His voice and was never afraid to step forth in new paths when she was sure of His guidance.

The Lord granted her many for her harvest for Him, and in the glory, many will meet her and call her blessed.

May her "Testimony" lead many to follow in her steps, surrendering all to the Master, and following Him wherever He goeth.

Edith M Brown

INTRODUCTION

"**I**'VE STARTED A NEW BOOK!" She was standing at the end of Peace Cottage verandah, Jainagar, waiting for us in the early morning as we came across from Zion Cottage. "You have begged me so long to write about myself, and I think it's time I gave my testimony, so I am writing it—"and she flashed at us her inimitable smile that all who knew her love to remember.

Inimitable, too, her way of writing. She always wrote just as she talked, in a style all her own. The text has been left as she wrote it, and reading, we can almost hear again her telling it all, naturally, intimately, straight from her heart to our hearts.

"This is my last Will and Testimony!" she repeated constantly in late months, as she came away from her desk to join us.

And between the beginning and the end?

One can hardly conceive how this book has been contested from first to last. Only a few chapters were written when the author was seized with a distressing illness, and she, and we, recognized in it an attempt of the Enemy to crush out life, that these words might never be written.

In August she came back to us here for a place a little less enervating than Gorakhpur: and it was only the Lord's goodness that carried her through the humid heat of the next months; but between preparing for England, and quite a thousand and one daily interruptions, which only those who live in the East can understand, this book was written.

"I do not want anyone to miss the Way!" she exclaimed more than once. "Is that clear?"--after reading a newly written piece--"I do want as many as possible to find Him"-- "Will that do?"

After she had entered into the Glory, and met her Beloved, the remainder of the precious MSS. was handed over to be typed; a fire broke out in the house where it was; another bid, me thinks, of the Enemy to end its usefulness--the manuscript was saved.

Like the *Acts of the Apostles,* this book was not finished, and yet, like that, the works it writes of are still going on: there is no end till we are all gathered Yonder.

And the Message is complete, is it not, for all who will receive it? May it be that more fruit will abound through her who yet speaketh from the Land that is Fairer than Day, than ever abounded in the years she was here in our midst.

May we find, as she did, each step of the way, the exquisite, preciousness of his Presence, as her verse below expresses:

I am my own Beloved's
And all there is of me
Is His, for now and always,
His only will I be.
In love and understanding
Down from His home on high,
He came to draw me to Him,
And He has brought me nigh,
So nigh, I feel His heartbeats,
So near, He breathes on me,
So close, His arms can hold me,
Through all eternity.
I'm living in His Presence,
At home in love's own place,
The past with all its wanderings

Has gone--there's not a trace.
For love has bound me to Him
And love has filled my soul;
Love now controls my spirit
And He has made me whole.
And I shall sing the love songs
To Him Who loveth me,
Taught by His Holy Spirit
In love's own ecstasy.
In love I have been ransomed,
In love He conquered me,
In love I am with Jesus,
I live--just His to be.--M.W.B.
Elise Page
The Gorakhpur Nurseries' Fellowship
Gorakhpur, U.P., India

TESTIMONY

❧ I ❧

EARLY YEARS

"THOU SHALT REMEMBER that thou wast a bondman in the land of Egypt, and the lord thy God redeemed thee." (Deut. 15.15).

"Thou shalt remember all the way which the Lord thy God led thee these forty years." (Deut.8:2)

"Jesus said: "When He (the Holy Spirit) is come, He will testify of Me.....and ye also because ye have been with Me." (John 15.26, 27)

Thou shalt remember, Thou shalt remember. He shall testify of Me, and ye also, because ye have been with me.

Early Years

I had a birthday last month, and I awoke one morning to find that I had spent half of my life at Gorakhpur--for it was thirty-six years since I first arrived there. It is about time that I gave my testimony, and yet, when I begin to think about it, I am speechless with wonder and amazement that God called me to be a missionary, and I must testify.

How can I begin? First of all, let me answer some of the questions so often put to me.

No--I was not born in a Christian home, I was not taught to

say prayers at my mother's knee, and I never saw anyone read the Bible or kneel to pray in my childhood home.

My parents had their own ideas formed through suffering they received at the hand of others, and they adhered to them, and no child of theirs was baptized. A friend once asked "Why this omission?" and my father answered: "People make solemn promises when children are christened: do they keep them?" So no babies from our home were carried into church for any ceremony, but we were a happy family living in unity.

My mother believed in love, and she expended it to its fullest limit on her children, and made home beautiful for us, and my father was the most understanding man I ever met, and yet, I often heard people say that we were a "godless lot."

No Church--no Chapel--no Religion!

The youngest of the family, and not easy to manage, the people who looked on said, "There is not a serious thought in her head;" but they did not know everything, for I did have serious thoughts and my mind wandered in realms foreign to the family-- great and vital questions would persist, but they were well hidden behind the laughter and fun-loving exterior. However, darkness under the bedclothes is a grand thinking ground, and there I sought to penetrate the secrets of some of the people I saw--and-- always there was one face radiant and calm that arrested me by its beauty.

I was a girl of eighteen, and she was about ten years older. I had known her all my life, and although she was a Christian, she had never once mentioned the name of Jesus to me. Why?

Because my parents had asked her not to do so, and she kept her promise, but she carried "the Unseen Presence," and although I did not recognize it, He was drawing me--yes, me, a rank unbe-liever--by the cords of His love, and because she was so different from everybody else I saw or knew I set out to find the secret, and saw a great deal of her.

She was a Wesleyan, and went to a Class meeting and to Chapel twice every Sunday. Everything about her spoke of beauty, and her gracious manner when she bent to speak just lifted me up and made me want something I hadn't got.

In an off-hand manner I watched and waited, always laughing and making fun to hide that something that was awakening in me, and which I found so difficult to control, for I was afraid of it. I bought a Bible. "This is what the Christians believe," I said to myself, getting seriously to work to find out, asking if it were true! Thus I began at Genesis 1.

It was an amazing start, and not at all the dull book I had been told it was. It rang with truth, every page was full of interest, and no one was ever more thrilled by a novel or romance.

I was interested in the people and thrilled by their experiences. When I came to Daniel, the story of the three men walking in the fiery furnace kept me awake all one night, having been called away before I could finish it, and the questions in my heart were, "Would they be allowed to die? Would no one help them? Would no one save them?" These filled my anxious mind, and I got up early next morning to read to the end of the wonderful story of deliverance. There was *one*, walking with them in the fire, and somehow I knew it was God.

Afraid to read any further for some time, I read that story over and over again until it burned in my soul. For the first time in my life, I believed God and I was afraid in the dark.

Weeks went by, and months too, and I was still reading through the Bible, and for the third time in the New Testament, and somehow as I read the Gospel story, *one* Person stood out, alone, and I read it over again. Each time I read the story I was entranced by Him and His ways: He was so different from everybody else, He was royal, and yet so humble, His kindness was alluring, His understanding perfect, and yet, whatever He did was criticized, misunderstood, and condemned by the religious people of the day. The priests and Pharisees hadn't a good word to say for Him, they sought opportunity to frustrate all His efforts, and the strongest feelings within me were anger against those people and sympathy for the One Who went about doing good.

They called Him "Jesus of Nazareth," and my heart went out after Him, and I read on. Then one day I stopped--to face the situation --for I had just read the wonderful words recorded in the Gospel according to John: "Henceforth I call you not servants, for the servant knoweth not what his Lord doeth; but, I have called you friends." I had read it before: I read it again and marveled at the significance: then I turned back the sacred pages, and tried to count up just how long those men had been with Him--was it three years? I sat to think. "Oh, I wish I could be His friend," my heart said, and then I began to wonder if it were possible. Oh, if only--if only--but I decided that day that I would try to be good for three years, and do all I could to find out the things that He would like and perhaps--yes, perhaps--I held my heart to consider--perhaps--He would see and call me His friend.

I was nineteen of age--thus I started. I told my father that I was going to try to be good and one day hoped to be a Christian! He listened with suspicion and his only remark was: "We shall see."

My brothers were skeptical, and assured me that I was not cut out to be a Christian: I laughed too much and made fun of everything. They said there was no solemnity about me, and no one realized that in reading the Bible I had touched the living Word, and it was something I could not get away from. `Most of all, I had seen the Saviour of the World with His disciples, and oh, how I wanted to join them.

I had no sense of sin and no understanding of my need, and yet, and yet, oh, how I wanted Him, and the record in the Gospels filled all my vision, and all my thoughts were how to get to know Him.

Since my eyes were fixed on Jesus
I lost sight of all beside,
and decided to give up the world and all the attractions it held for my pleasure-loving nature. I was preparing for a County Ball, but did not go: I refused to go to the theater: I looked around and made my own code of morals, and deciding that self-denial was my need, I practiced it. The friend with the radiant face said that I

laughed too much, so I tried to be sober. I was in earnest, but knew it would not be easy. I couldn't count the cost, for I did not know it, but frivolity gave way to serious thinking, and I stuck to the Bible and tried to learn the way to live. I had no questions about the Author: everything I read proved it. It was the Word of God and I had no doubts about anything in it.

Of course, there was much that I could not understand, and that made me more sure that it was the Word of the Lord God Almighty and a great reverence was born within me. I had respect for His Word: I wouldn't have dared to criticize it.

Of course, I made no secret of my intention to be a Christian, and having found the Bible to be so very interesting, I tried to persuade people to read it--and they did. I was gripped by the Book, and soon discovered that it had a wonderful power that could not be described, that "it could be better felt than telt"--it was there and the Word began to work.

I went with my radiant friend to her Class meeting, and there came face to face with the real thing. The members were men and women who worked in the mills. They started work at 6 o'clock every morning, and left it at 6 o'clock in the evening, and about twelve of them were at the Class every Wednesday night by 7:30.

The leader was a saddler by trade and had a shop in the village, and he was a lover of souls. The meeting began with a hymn, prayer and reading of the Scriptures. Then each in turn was asked to give his or her testimony, and I was amazed at the reality of it all. They lived the life, they talked of God as a personal Friend Who had helped them every day, and they told us details of how and when He had done it. I was thrilled by their stories, but the second half of the meeting was given up to prayer--it was then I was awed and calmed into reverence. Their prayers were as simple as themselves--just a heart-pouring out to Some One Who wanted to hear them. Two of them (they were man and wife) seemed to make a big difference, for the atmosphere was changed from the ordinary everyday into the celestial, and a solemn hush came like a wave over the Class when they talked with the Unseen Presence.

Now (after all these years thinking it over), I believe it was really that "their cry went up and God came down," and when we left the Class meeting everybody looked refreshed.

I could only go sometimes, but drank deeply of reality, and saw much that I had never dreamed was for me. These people welcomed me into their midst: but I was not one of them-and I knew it.

As I read the Bible, its truths were unfolded and the mysterious way that leads to God was opened to me: and when I read, "he that believeth and is baptized shall be saved," I knew there was something to be done, but how? was the question.

I spoke to my father about baptism, and he was very definite that such a step was impossible and not to be thought of by me, so the subject was closed for the time being. In the midst of everything, God took my mother, and I was stranded, stripped of a love I was sure of whatever happened, and speechless with the stroke. I stood to face life without her, and almost before I realized it, He took my sister, then two others very near and very dear were taken, and I knew it was God, and I was dumb in His presence. I had nothing to say, absolutely nothing: my heart was awake to the reality of His power: He was truly Almighty, able to do anything: and I felt small and not worth noticing: yet, the thirst remained and I pursued my quest.

I read the Bible consecutively, and sought and sought and sought: nothing daunted my ardor, nothing kept me from seeking, and yet I did not find what met my soul's true need. Four months after my twenty-first birthday, I left home and went to stay with a friend three hundred miles away, and for the first time in my life I was in a Christian home, where there was family prayer daily, and each and all, the servants included, went to Church every Sunday. A new life opened before me: but it was only the beginning.

I asked questions from one who knew the way, and was guided to the path of obedience. I soon realized that the commandments of God are meant to be obeyed. I asked, "how?" for some things seemed so impossible, and the answer given was, "try and see." I did as I was told, and problems were eased, seeming impossibilities were not difficult when I made up my mind to do them! "God expects obedience" my friend said, and so I learned the way that leads to the path of righteousness and obeyed the commands He gave to me.

After a time, I moved on to a lovely seaside town on the South Coast. I wanted to do something that would help others--I was free to serve--but how? I thought of nursing as a career, but no one would hear of it. "No hospital would take you," they said. The strain of the mental suffering had sapped most of my strength. Just then a friend asked me to stay with her for two weeks, and I "could help her in her work among young women" she said. Only converted from a very worldly life three months before: she was fresh in her endeavor, and like a fire, her enthusiasm kindled my zeal afresh.

I still hoped to be a nurse, but every advance toward that course was met by the reminder that it needed more strength than I had. "Wait a little longer" was the advice; "stay here and help me for the present," and because I was wanted I stayed on for years. I did not know then that it was a preparation for the life that was to be. I learned order and what selflessness really is: that Christianity is not talk, it is life, and that if you live it, it is no secret: everybody knows it who lives with you.

I learned to go regularly to the House of God to worship, and that Sunday is very specially God's own day, there being many promises made to those who keep the day holy. Someone put a paper in my hand with a few directions written on it, of which one was "Careful Observance of Sunday," and I signed it with my name in full. Among other directions were two--the first was "Daily Reading of the Bible," and the second, "Praying for Others." Those two settled my mind as to the course I must take.

Sunday became what it ought to be--God's own special day. The Church was a special meeting-place. The morning service was filled with worshipers, and in the afternoon my friend took me to a Bible Class, where I sat among two hundred girls and young women listening to teaching such as I had never dreamed of. The Bible was an open Book, and the sound of the turning of the leaves to find references by everybody present was like the sound of the wind in the trees! It was a great experience, and I sat and looked and pondered, and took to heart the lessons given. The Church was filled to capacity every Sunday morning, and in the evening, chairs were brought into the aisles and put in every possible space, only to be occupied immediately.

The singing was grand, everybody seemed to have a voice, and as the padre had said that the responses were to be said or sung, they were given like the sound of many waters.

After the evening service, those of the congregation who wanted to hear more were asked to stay, and there were generally more than five hundred whose hearts heeded the call. They waited with others to respond, and there must have been much rejoicing in heaven over sinners finding their way to God there.

The quietness in the Church, and the calm delivery of the message, made it easy to hear the still small voice. I sat and waited and joined with all that--one among them, but not of them--and I couldn't tell why--till something happened.

I went away from there for a month's change, presumably to help to comfort a girl who was lonely and desolate in a new place, and we went to visit the sick in the little local Cottage Hospital. The Matron asked me to sing for her patients, which I was only too glad to do. I went again and again, but there was something about that Matron that was peculiarly pleasing: she looked absolutely satisfied, she spoke in a low voice, and her speech was other-worldly. "I wonder if she really is satisfied?" I said to myself. "She looks it: I'd like to ask her. People talk about being satisfied, but I have never seen anyone who really is. I think I will ask her: but it took more courage than I had, so I waited for another opportunity, and every day for a week the same thing happened. Then, one day, I thought it was my last day there, and felt very desperate. I walked up and down the corridor with her, trying to screw up courage to ask the vital question which was so personal. At last, when the daylight was fading, I ventured: "I want to ask you something." She stopped. "Yes, dear, what is it?" she asked, and I blurted out: "Are you satisfied?" She stood in amazement at my question. "I am," she replied, "why do you ask that question?" "You look it," was my blunt reply, and overcome by the courage I had worked up for the ordeal, I lost control and I cried like a child. "Come to my room," she said and I began to tell her as we went. "There is no need for me to cry. I don't know why I do it," and yet there was something within me that had flung the door open and I could not control myself. My eyes were suddenly opened, and I realized that all I had given up, all I had tried to do and be--all--everything was as nothing. Somehow I had missed the way, although I had left all to find Jesus--and she quietly read words from the Book. They went over me I was too miserable to understand. I had reached the end of my tether, and holding my face in my hands sobbed out: "I didn't know and I have missed the way. I am lost." She came and knelt by me and I knelt too. Conviction of sin swept over my soul. No one had said anything about it, no one had told me of my need. I had done everything I knew to be a Christian. I had left all, given up all that I thought was worldly, separated myself from old companions, joined with those who were professed Christians--I was changed, and yet, had never been born again, never been convicted of sin until now. The whole of my past intense trying was only a miserable failure I had not found the way, I was lost; and, because this little Matron was so filled with the Holy Spirit, He could do His work and He convicted me of sin. I discovered there that what I had thought could be changed, was really sin, requiring to be confessed, forgiven and put away.

I realized that sin is sin and not shortcoming. I was not a Christian after all: I had missed the way: I had depended on my own doings, my own decisions, and depended even on what I thought. I wanted the Highest and the Best, and was looking where it could not be found. I knelt in misery until a late hour, and then went home to my friends, going straight to my own room to be alone: I wanted to pray but I couldn't. I was in the depths and no sleep came to my relief: I knew that I was lost: the sin of unbelief held me captive and I have never once said that I was sorry: and oh, how humbled and ashamed I was as I thought about it. I got out of bed to confess all I knew, and the words of a hymn they sang at the Bible Class on Sunday afternoon came to my mind and helped me to pray:

Father, I have wandered from Thee,
Often has my heart gone astray,
Crimson do my sins seem to me—
Water cannot wash them away
Jesus, to that fountain of Thine,
Leaning on Thy promise I go!
Cleanse me by Thy washing divine,
And I shall be whiter than snow.

And I prayed on, but it was not until the third day that I saw the light. I had opened my Bible in search of comfort and my eyes were riveted on one little sentence: "Ye must be born again." The old question, "How?" was persistently repeated within me. Then I thought I would ask Him to tell me how--and--He did. And I knelt again and waited to see what He would do.

The past would not let me forget. I was held in misery until I cried, "Oh, Lord, save me or I perish"--and something dropped from me--the chains that held me down disappeared: the Blood of Jesus Christ, God's Son, had cleansed my heart from sin.

"Is this being born again?" I asked myself, and peace which passeth understanding filled my soul: I knew that I was forgiven. I knew that I was born again, a new life was flowing within, and I went back to the Matron in the hospital, and she took her Bible and read these words to me: "He will subdue our iniquities, and will cast all our sins in the depths of the sea." We knelt while she prayed, and I heard a voice saying: "Forgetting those things which are behind, and reaching forth unto those things which are before, I press toward the mark for the prize of the high calling of God in Christ Jesus." I rose and faced her. The transaction was done, I was a new creation, and I went back to the friend in the town by the sea to tell her all. The following Sunday morning the text in the sermon was--"Forgetting the things that are behind." There! It was repeated, and I took the significance of it to my heart. I knew it had to be done, and my hands stretched out to the future. All this gave me a great understanding of what it is to miss the way, and I set out to help anybody and everybody I could to start at the beginning and to waste no time trying, but to get into the realty, to begin at the beginning, to be born again. Suddenly I realized that I had found my quest: Jesus stood beside me, saying "Follow Me, and I will make you a fisher of men"

I felt like falling on my face before Him, but it was a public place and so I just whispered His Name. "Jesus, Jesus," I repeated softly, overcome with the Presence, "Let me love Thee," I whispered, and He wrapped me round in His love and made me feel His forever.

Looking over the calendar, I discovered that it was exactly three years since that great decision was made to set out to try and be good and to find out what would please Jesus. And He had not only saved me, He had told me what He would make of me! I was accepted in the Beloved, and glory filled my soul. When I read the words, "Ye are My friends if ye do whatsoever I command you," I made up my mind to obey.

A new life opened out to me, and I saw visions of what might be. The striking thing to me was the understanding I had when listening to the sermon on Sunday. There was a special service each Friday morning for the deepening of the spiritual life. I went several times, but it was beyond me, so I stayed away; but after my experience in the little hospital, all things had become new. To my surprise, I knew what they were talking about, and I opened my eyes wide to see the land of far distances.

The possibilities in life seemed beyond our ken, but the padre held his hands out and pleaded with us to receive. I drank deeply of God's Spirit.

I shall never forget the first time I heard anyone talk about what is called "The Second Coming." It was Advent Sunday, the

Church was packed, and as we came out after the service, I said to some others: "You would think Jesus is really coming again the way the parson talks--isn't he confident?" "He is coming again," was the answer in a very surprised tone. "Are you sure?" I asked. "Of course I am," was the answer. I waited until I got home to ask my friend, and she assured me that what the padre had said was all true--Jesus literally is coming again, and she opened her Bible to read those precious words, "Behold I come quickly." "What do you think it means?" she asked, and I answered promptly: "Oh I thought that if I were in any trouble, He would come quickly to my help--nothing more--nothing less."

She took my hand and led me to a chair where we could kneel together and she asked the Holy Spirit to reveal this truth to me. I felt it was true, and yet, too good to be true: but as I thought of it a rapturous joy filled my soul, and that "Blessed Hope" was born within me. Now there came to me a realization that, although I read the Bible, I did not understand it. Holy men of old had written words which God had given, and there still must be holy men who knew the meaning of what they read. That morning's sermon had proved it to me, and I knew that I needed teaching. It came to me like a flash that I must not go on as I had done: the Scriptures were not given for private interpretation, and that was what I had done from the beginning. So I bought a book called *How to Study Your Bible,* written by D. L. Moody, and began in earnest to learn from those who knew. It was a challenge to my sincerity, but from that time I began to study the Bible. Before then, I had read it, and read it every day, but to study it--to read, mark, learn, and inwardly digest the words in Holy Writ, I did not know how: private interpretation had not led me to the under-standing I needed. I must learn from others, and here I was in a place where I could, if I would, and as I searched the Scriptures, I found hidden treasures.

That Advent Sunday service transformed my daily reading into a deep study of God's Word. That thing they call "The Blessed Hope" was born within me, and it came to stay. It has been the inspiration of my life, and since then I have measured events in the light of His Coming.

The Bible Class on Sunday afternoon was no longer a mystery, neither did I feel outside. I knew that I was one of them, yet no one spoke a word about it, and it gave me a radiant assurance that all was well. I belonged to the family of God and I felt enriched by belonging.

The little book I had begun with--*How to Study Your Bible,* gave me a taste for the real thing, so I bought a *Cruden's Concordance* and set to work in earnest. When I went to meetings my heart always said: "Tell me more about Jesus."

Bible study was not satisfying, for I always wanted more! And I grasped at every opportunity where I could learn how to study in real earnest. I could read and I could learn, but when I began to study the Bible all my powers were extended, and the habit grew. I bought books and read them, and they helped me, but comparing Scripture with Scripture helped me most, and I stuck to that method. The little Greek Testament I had became increasingly precious. I read it with the heart of a pioneer searching for hidden treasures; every day meant a little progress in the voyage of discovery, and what I found I shared with those near me. As the secrets were revealed, I had to tell someone. I gathered with others, who wanted to know, and we sat together with our Bibles, reading, marking, and learning more of the most wonderful Book in the world, and my life was enriched.

It couldn't stop at that: others gathered, and as I talked about Jesus, they opened their hearts and came to Him. Then there were meetings to which bright young school girls came to search with me, and the teacher who brought them was the first to say: "I have found Him here, and I have dedicated my life to Him." She went to distant lands to tell others.

There was a class of children, about fifty of them meeting every Saturday, and they asked me to help there, but the children helped me much more than they ever knew. I learned to stand on my own feet, I listened to their opinions of others, and their criticisms were very searching and more often than not they touched the vital point. I didn't know how to repress them: I made friends with them instead, and we talked things over together until we met on common ground. They told me what they wanted, and I tried to get it for them. I told them what I wanted and they sat quietly to listen. Sometimes a little hand was slipped into mine when the meeting was over and we started off together while I listened to their heart-pourings as we walked, and I learned how real is the hunger and thirst for God in the hearts of children: and oh, how glad I was that I knew the Friend of little children and could introduce them to Him.

Several years of that life in the beautiful town by the sea, and then we moved on to scenes far different, but the same need was there, and we settled down and faced the situation.

The early years of my life had not prepared me for that work, for how could I know the Scriptures and understand the teaching as those who had been in it and learned from their childhood? When a tree is grown, it is not easy to bend: I was grown up before I knew anything of the reality of the Christian life--but I did know what it was to be without Christ, and as I thought things over, I knew that I could make friends with those who were born as I was, indifferent to the claims of God, and the remembrance of what He said to me when I was born again gripped me. "Follow Me, and I will make you fishers of men" became the real thing. I knew that if I really and truly did follow Him, He would make me. It was not something to learn from a book. *He would make me.* He said so, and I sought with all my heart to follow. I had much to learn, for victory over sin and self was a big problem: nothing was easy, and my failures were very disappointing to me: but oh, His patience! It was wonderful and only a miracle kept me in the narrow way; it was so difficult, I felt so unable, but it mattered to Him what happened to me. I learned that it was not only a Mighty Saviour, able to save even me, He was the understanding Jesus and He said: "I came not to condemn but to save." I should have gone under, disappointed in the way, had not something happened, and I went out to meet it.

Someone casually said that young girls who lived and worked in the town were losing their best in their off-duty time. They were tired of wandering on the sea-front, and went to sit in the shelters, where they met those who were there only to ruining them. There seemed no one to help, so I went out about 9:30 or 10 o'clock every night to be where they were, make friends and bring them home with me for supper and home comforts.

Their lives were barren and loveless and full of drudgery. They didn't see the danger they were in until they were caught in the trap and it was too late. The stories they told me urged me to greater endeavor, and before long we had a number sitting round the fire talking out their hearts. They had escaped the snare, and it seemed the least we could do was to kneel and thank the Saviour before we parted about midnight.

Out of those seeking and finding came a band of young women saved to serve.

There were other calls, but that little company stands out in my memory as brands snatched out of the fire. Among other gems I found were those who were brought up as I was, and with the same outlook on life. Their opinions of the Christians were no credit, and I asked one of them what she expected. "Sincerity at least," was the reply. "And what have you done to help them?" was my question to them. A little curl of the lip, and a toss of the head and a pause, then—"They profess so much and, and--" "And what?" I asked. "Oh, you don't know what it means to me who have no religion to see so much profession and so little practice," was the next remark. "I've no patience with religious people." But I held my ground and said: "I know exactly what you mean, for I have been where you are and lived the same life, and when I began to seek this life I thought I would never find it, but here I am and I know the way and I know Him Who is the Way. Why don't you seek the Lord while He may be found and call upon Him while He is near, and then show some of these people you are talking about what the real thing is? Then, you could practice what you know: perhaps they do not know, and you could help them: folk don't always know all there is to know even when they are born in a Christian home!"

We got very friendly over the matter, and one day she came to see me to tell me that she had bought a Bible and had begun to read it, and would I tell her how to begin the Christian life?

We had great times together--she belonged to a godless set, and she talked with them and they were allured by the change in her, and several started to go to Church on Sunday. I called on them, and they talked *ad lib*.

And were quite surprised at the end when I asked: "Would you like me to pray about that?" They were not slow to discover that what they thought was rock for their feet was just sinking sand.

I still lived with the friend I first went to in the beautiful town by the sea, and she counted nothing too much trouble or too big a burden if only she could help others in this place.

Life was full and very busy every day, then suddenly she was taken from me, and I held my heart and waited--crushed and bleeding, not knowing what the future held. I went to friends in the country to wait and see.

A relative of my hosts was staying there for a holiday. She was a Mildmay deaconess, and one day she said to me: "I wish you could come to Mildmay, we need you there."

The surprise was almost too much for me and I asked: "How could I live up to the standards you have talked about?" She smiled and answered, "Come and see," and I set to work to make any excuse possible to evade any more talk about going to Mildmay! That was far too high for me, I was sure. The thought of the exacting life there made me say over and over again: "That is not for me, I am not fitted for that life"; for in spite of all I had gone through, I was not yet ready for anything. But one morning a letter came, inviting me there for a month. My friend who was taken so suddenly from me was a friend of the one who wrote: she knew all, and she asked me to go to her there I clutched my heart, girded the loins of my mind, and went.

They say that first impressions last, yet how could I give them? They are deeply set in my heart. It was more than a new place, it was a new world. Over the entrance were the words declaring: "There they dwelt with the King for His work."

"Could anything be more wonderful?" I said to myself, I was taken to "the powers that be" to be introduced, and settled in for my visit.

Lord, give me a Vision
"Where there is no vision,
The people perish"--Prov.19:18
Lord, give me a vision,
A vision of Thee,
Lest people should perish,
Who live around me.
A vision I pray thee,
Straight from above,
To win those around me
By Thy mighty love.
Lord, give me a vision,
Of what love can do,
I give myself to Thee,
To carry me through.
Of how I can do it,
In love's perfect way,
A vision I pray thee, Lord, give me to-day.

2

MILDMAY

AND NOW, I am at Mildmay. How can I describe the place? It was a revelation to me: so many women coming in and going out, everyone with something to do and busy doing it. There were no leisurely movements, and no hurry either. It was life dignified, holy and purposeful. Yes. "There they dwelt with the King for His work": it was not mere words, it was a fact, and I was looking on, marveling that so many women were gathered together to go out to districts where sin and poverty were rife, to seek and to save that which was lost. The Deaconess House was built on to the Conference Hall that seated over a thousand people. There were lecture rooms, a big dining-room, a very spacious drawing-room, and many other rooms, and higher up were little bedrooms that were sanctuary for the deaconesses, and there were other houses in the compound for still more deaconesses.

There was an orphanage for girls, and a plain little building they called "The Illumination Room," where cards and calendars painted and illuminated by those belonging to Mildmay were printed and exhibited for sale. They went all over the world, for every card had a text from the Bible and every calendar had a message from God.

There was a little hospital always full of patients, and staffed by keen Christian women ministering to the sick. There was another hospital, much bigger, in the slums of the East End, and numbers of missionaries were trained there. It was a world within a world, and I was taken round to see everything and to drink of its spirit.

Every day in the week was full up except one, as every deaconess had a rest day away from the districts where she served.

I went about from Mission to Mission seeing all, talking with the people, hearing amazing stories. I was up against poverty, sin and degradation. It was wonderful to see how these women tackled it--nothing seemed to overwhelm them. Nothing seemed to daunt them, and nothing was too much trouble if only those sunken people could be saved. I saw gems that had been snatched from the enemy of souls, men and women who were once drunkards, and who had been saved in the Mission Halls. I met and talked with men who had served their time in jail, and now--because of the love that sought them, they were brought into the fold, and you would never guess what their past had been, because it was obliterated by the light in their faces. I met them in the House of God, "forgiven much, they loved much."

Every day seemed more wonderful than the day before. Life was real, life was earnest, and full of purpose: and I struggled to keep up with the aggressiveness day by day, as I went with the deaconesses to see what God was doing in the slums of London. It was the hardest month I ever remembered, fuller than anything I ever dreamed of; getting to know what it is to be poor.

I was very tired, but my vision of life was changed. The need was greater than I had ever seen. Sin and degradation flouted one in the face, but there was comradeship among the poorest of the poor that compelled attention and shamed the respectable looker-on. Again I say, life was real--sham could not live in such an atmosphere of stark reality, and I was humbled with respect for the poverty-stricken people who lived in the slums. There life was lived at a cost that could not be measured by any standards I had known before.

The stories I heard were heart-rending, though the people told them as if such happenings were the most usual thing in the world. The place these people called *"Home"* was usually one room, where husband and wife and sometimes three, four, or more children lived. What chance had they for the decencies of life? If sin abounded was it any surprise? They walked about the streets because they had nowhere else to go, and they got into trouble because they had nothing very particular to do: and oh, how I longed to help them!

The month was drawing to a close and I had been too busy even to think of the future, the *"now"* was so full up and my mind was so absorbed with what I saw and heard. One day I was walking down the street, when suddenly a drunken woman reeled around the corner, and I staggered at the impact. She steadied herself against the wall and tried to articulate words, and then swayed. The deaconess with me just caught her before she fell, and without any introduction she looked at me, threw her arms around me and called me "darling." It was the surprise of my life that I was not frightened. All my heart went out to this drunken woman, and I drew her arm through mine as we stood for a moment until we got our bearings, and I listened to loving words of sisterly care, spoken in tenderness--as if it mattered to my companion that the woman was drunk. There was not one word of condemnation! We took the drunkard to her home, steadied between us. Sobered a bit by the walk, she reeled into her kitchen.

"Is that what being a deaconess means?" I asked my companion.

"I don't understand," she replied. "Well--what you have just done."

"That is nothing," she said as she went into a little shop to buy coffee, and then we went back and she put the tin kettle on the gas-ring, and very soon the woman was drinking a cup of strong coffee, muttering between the sips that she was not drunk: she had only had a little too much and she was glad to see "Sister."

"Think of being able to do that!" I said to myself. "Poor woman, what can have driven her to such depths of degradation?": I questioned as we walked to the train to take us back to the Deaconess House. My companion said, "I must go early to-morrow morning to find out how she is." I couldn't forget. I wanted to help those who were down and out, sunken in sin and sodden in drink, but how?

I had never seen such people, or such abject poverty; and cheerful drunkards! Sin was something to be covered over, and sin was only sin when it was found out.

I went with a different deaconess every day, and never once did I hear an impatient word spoken to the people of the districts. I saw them sit or stand and listen to outpourings, and I heard them pray definite prayers for those who had opened their heart to Him, and I knew they expected an answer.

After a month of all that, I was interviewed by the Head of Affairs, and I came away with some papers to read and a number of questions to answer that needed clear thinking and exact phrasing.

The sequel was that I stayed on and was accepted by the powers that be, and went to the East End with a very senior deaconess to be initiated into the life and work and introduced to the people.

I could scarcely believe it. When I got to the Mission House and saw that there was, and was told what to do, I started off with a list of names and addresses, to visit the absentees from the Mothers' Meeting and "tomorrow," said my senior, "I will show your district to you." So I started out.

I lost my heart to the people on my first contact with them. Their need was so desperate and they were so cheerful in their poverty! Every house seemed to be full of little children scrambling over whatever there was, and beside the baby in arms, there were babies clinging to the mother's garments while she swayed her body in her endeavor to stand up and talk on the doorstep. "What a life! What grit!" I thought, while the woman poured out her history to my listening heart. Her last baby was born four days ago, and she was up and doing and making excuses for what she could not do! Such as the introduction to me of the brave mothers of the East End of London! They won my respect right away. The next day I was taken out and shown the streets and the houses not far from the Mission Hall. "This is your district," my senior said, as we stood at the end of a very long road with many side-turnings, and each house accommodating several families. "Every house must be visited and every family in every house." I then received an address book to be filled in by me as I learned the names of the people and the number of their house, and another small book to write down things to be remembered. I put them in a little bag with my pocket Bible and started off. "This is my district," I said again, and I knocked at the first door in the long street, and the door opened just a little way. "What do you want?" said the woman.

"I just called to see you," I answered.

"Well, I've no time," she snapped, and slammed the door. I stood by the shut door for a moment to recover from my surprise, and then took a few steps to the next, but it was not answered. I saw a woman standing in the street, so I greeted her with a smile and told her that I was going to visit her if she lived anywhere near. She laughed and asked, "Whatever for?" "I want to make friends," I answered. She laughed loud and long, and called some jeering words to a woman opposite, and I walked to the next house.

"No one at home," someone shouted, but I saw faces peering behind the curtains. They had caught the fashion of people who know better and declared they were not at home when they did not wish to have a visitor. So I passed on. Every door that first day was closed to me: no one opened and no one wanted to be friends, but I had been told that this was *my* district, and I said, "These people *are my* people," and they didn't want me—what was I to do?

I returned to the Mission House, and sat down to a meal with three others who had been visiting their people, and had much to say about them, and I told them of my failure.

"Just keep on," said one next to me. "Keep on and let me know if I can do anything to help you" and loneliness in failure vanished when we knelt to pray.

Everything was so definite: everybody prayed to the point and when they prayed for me I felt that it mattered to them: they were concerned about my failure, and the evening service in the Mission Hall drew me closer to them.

Day after day I visited doors and doorsteps, but no one asked me in until one day I came suddenly upon a group of women standing with their arms akimbo--each one carried a jug in her hand which she tried to hide under her apron. Of course, I saw without appearing to notice and laughed with them. I had caught them unawares so I just stated that "I had called and no one answered." which brought forth more laughter. "I am a bit tired of walking up and down this street," I said. "Won't you come to the Mothers' Meeting this afternoon? And the excuses they made were as those recorded in Scripture--but I stood on.

"I think I'll go and make a cup of tea," said the stoutest lady of the group--and someone nodded at the jug. We were almost next door to a "pub," so it was quite easy to slip in there and get the beer they longed for: besides, the drink could be got without fire or any trouble to themselves--so beer was the daily morning tea. "I'll give you a cup of tea if you will come to the Mothers' Meeting," I said: for a cup of tea and two biscuits were always given to everyone there.

Then the leader of the group spoke up: "I'll go in and make a cup of tea for the lady, and then I'll come out and tell you." She beckoned me with her head and I followed her in.

I had spent most of the night before in prayer, for I was very desperate. I could *not* make friends with these people: they would not have me, yet, I said to myself, "these people are my people, and I want my God to be their God." Thus I prayed in the night,

telling God that I would do anything if only He would save them--
and lo! here I was sitting in a very small kitchen near a table full of
dirty crockery, and the woman who beckoned me in was standing
with a tin teapot in her hand and filling it up to the brim with
water to put on to the gas-ring. There were plenty of used tea-
leaves in the pot, and when some tea dust was added to the boiling
mixture, I began to tremble. A big cup was washed, and wiped on a
towel used for many purposes, then a spoon dipped into a half-
empty tin of condensed milk and twice into a bowl of sugar, "to
make it sweet for me," she said. I begged against it, saying I did
not take sugar. "I wouldn't give it to you without sugar." she said,
"it would be like medicine," and she put the cup of hot liquor in
my hand." It will do you good," she assured me. "I'm sure you get
tired walking up and down this road: there is nothing like a cup
of tea!"

Well, I had said that I would do anything if only I could get in
with these people, and here was the answer, which I sipped--and
steadied myself.

To drink tea with them was to accept them and a proof that
they accepted me, but I never tasted such tea in my life, and
hurried away when my cup was emptied lest the after-effects
should be disastrous. As I went out, the East-ended called: "Come
again, Miss, come whenever you like, there will always be a
welcome for you, and a cup of tea!" That was my entrance into the
home of the people in my district, and again I said "These people
shall be my people," and I prayed that my God might be their God
too. It was as if something broke all through and doors opened
after that in an amazing manner. I went in and out and made
friends, and one by one the worst were saved, the respectable
converted, and the meetings increased in numbers. It would fill a
volume to tell all I saw the Lord do there.

We started a Club, ostensibly for lads, but they were really
young men from 16 to 26 years of age. Every one of them was a
Socialist and wore the red kerchief knotted round his neck: most

of them had been in jail, and they were a crowd to be managed. They gave us lively meetings, pinned us down to pray, and quickened our thinking powers. They had an answer for everything and asked hundreds of questions. Frequently they crowded round the Hall some time before the doors were opened, but we could not take more than eighty at a time in the Club, and even sometimes the noise was terrific. I learned a great deal there of life in Wormwood Scrubs, and their stories of the Sunday service and singing of the Psalms were revelations of doings in jail. They sang the tune, putting in their own words! If they recognized a friend and he stood behind singing the Psalms for the day—instead of the words in the Prayer Book, he sang: "Bill Sykes, what are you doing here?" and the other answered to the same tune. This is the way that they had conversation with each other and triumphed in their victory over the disadvantages of being in prison.

They loved the Club and came regularly and listened to the 10 minutes' address at the end, joining lustily in the hymns, singing what words they wanted to say to their neighbors: but, after I learned about the psalm singing in prison, I listened and watched faces, and one night we sang a chorus twenty-six times until they realized that we could go no further—the words in the book were to be sung. The atmosphere cleared, but we were a long time before there was a break, and it came on Sunday night, rather late. The services were over: we had just finished supper and were preparing to go upstairs, when there was a loud banging on the door and our landlady hurried to see what was the matter.

Three young men stood there, speechless.

"What do you want at this time of night?" she asked.

"We want the lady," they said, and the one with me jumped up to see what was needed, but before she could speak a voice said: "No—'tain't 'er, 'tis the fat 'un!" and I went to the door.

"What is it?" I asked, and the three came close to me, and one blurted out: "Can't stick it no longer, Miss." I looked on puzzled—then he repeated—"Can't stick it no longer, Miss: we've got to do something:" and then, like a flash, I knew, and said: "Wait a minute, I will open the doctor's door"--and that night those three were born again, and they opened the way for others.

I started a Bible Class for them which was well attended, and the most original meeting I ever had, for they talked, aired their opinions, gave out what they thought a Christian should do, and should *not* do, and I learned a great deal.

From those beginnings others came, and I look back and see a Church Warden, a Padre, a leader of a Men's Meeting, and a band of Christian men who once were just members of the Club, nothing more, nothing less and in classes they attended they stepped on the lowest rung of the ladder that took them to where they are to-day.

We started a Bible Class for the girls who worked in the factories. I learned more of what it means to be poor, and where poverty unrelieved takes a girl, and I set out to meet that. I visited them, made friends with them, and then asked them to come on Sunday afternoon, but I did not know that they had no Sunday clothes and that they set great store on hats! I learned that it is possible to hire whatever they wanted--sometimes we had rather a gay crowd--hats very much in evidence, displaying gorgeous feathers!!! As I got to know my girls, I learned how they got their clothing, and I started a "Savings Bank" to help them to possess their own. They could not save it themselves, so I did it for them, and it was a great day when there was enough money grown from two pennies and three pennies into what would buy the longed-for Sunday frock, and very soon the hats, too, were paid for, and their hardworking lives were cheered by the Sunday gathering.

They opened their hearts to the Lover of Souls as only girls can, and I saw them enter into newness of life. We studied the Bible together, joined the Scripture Union, and instead of walking the streets they walked to Church. I loved them, they enriched my life, and I was quite settled among them.

The papers given to me when my first month of Mildmay was over were duly filled in and signed with my name in full, and I became a member of the Community. It did not take long to discover that a deaconess dress and bonnet were a help and shelter in visiting some of the worst parts of the East End, and when I was told they were for me, I could not believe it. My measurements were taken, and one never-to-be-forgotten day I put on the deaconess dress, and cap on head, stood before the glass to survey myself, and then I knelt to pray, but I had not words—my heart was too full to find expression. I was overwhelmed at the thought that I should be called a deaconess, and I cried out my heart before Him Who had brought me to that. He understands a cry as a mother does the cry of her child that has no words to express itself, and then I prayed to be worthy of this great honor.

The next day I went to the East End clothed like those I went with, and wearing the bonnet that distinguished a Mildmay Deaconess.

I have heard many laughs and jeers about the wearing of bonnets by people who were training for Christian service, but no queen ever felt the solemnity of her crowning more than I did when I first had that bonnet put on my heard. It was my crowning day in the service of the King of kings, and I was to serve in honor, for his glory.

Before very long, I followed the usual routing, and slept four nights every week in the Mission House in the East End and three nights each week in Mildmay.

The rules and regulations were handed to me on a printed paper, which I read carefully, and decided that they were made to be kept. They caused no difficulty to me as I had a strong sense of duty and a great longing to be worthy of my high calling, but I felt very ignorant in this household of God. I remember standing one day by the tennis courts and saying, "Oh, I wish I had someone to teach me," and a voice answered, "Learn of Me," so I knew He would teach me.

Visiting the people regularly brought me very close to them. They earned their living in their tiny homes, making shoes, slippers, beading them, making underclothes for the best shops in the

West End embroidery was easy to them: dress shirts and other garments were made at so much a dozen, and even the gorgeous regalia for Masons. I never saw such gorgeous silks in such poor places anywhere else, and the women who made them could scarcely pause to eat: they couldn't afford to lose the time, their pay was so low: and yet, uncomplaining, they worked six days a week without a pause. I sat down with them and read a few verses to them, and when I asked, "Shall we pray?" they smiled, saying, "We have no time." So I sat with them at their tables and learned to make matchboxes, and after a time I ventured to say I had made so many we had time to pray now, and with a sigh of relief they knelt.

I think it was the novelty of kneeling that broke the ice. I got closer to them and tried to make them feel that Jesus loved them and wanted them: they thought it over, and when I called again, it was easier to talk.

They were very free and easy in their manner, and even though their subjects for conversation were not always what I liked, I listened to them and they then listened to me, and I watched to see the soul's awakening.

Mr. N------was very ill in bed with rheumatic fever, and I went to see him. To my dismay, he had no warm clothes and very little bedding, and I sat by his bedside and asked if there was anything I could do! His wife was doing the best she could, and there were seven children. The man could not move, and his body was full of pain: he looked in agony. He said there was nothing I could do: he was in regular work, but had nothing saved: his wife was bright and shining and very cheerful, but when I asked about a doctor, she looked glum. "Yes, the doctor came and he said that my husband must have flannel shirts to be wrapped in blankets, but where can I get flannel shirts and blankets from? We can't get ordinary things, we are too many. But" she continued, "the doctor said my husband would not get well unless he were kept very warm, so I am doing the best I can." She was, but I shivered as I sat in that little fire-less room, and I asked God to help them, and went back to

Mildmay to report to one of the deaconesses who had charge of cupboards that held clothes of every description to be given to people in need. She listened with understanding sympathy and opened a cupboard. Yes--she could help she had two grey flannel shirts. She folded them up and gave them to me, and next day the sick man bit his lip and his wife wiped the tears from her eyes as I knelt at his bedside to thank God for providing this help and comfort: and oh! how I blessed Mildmay for this practical Christianity.

The man was a Socialist and had no leanings for Church or the Mission Hall, but these two flannel shirts spoke to his heart and they helped him in his pain, and he began to ask questions about Mildmay. The Hall in my district had its own Medical Mission, and I got help from there for him, and little by little he opened up, and his bravado faded away. I read the Scriptures to him, and his interest grew, till one day I asked him if he had ever thought of the words the Lord Jesus said: "Come unto Me all ye that labor and are heavy laden and I will give you rest"? "Yes, I have thought about them," he answered, "a fellow who stood on a box in Victoria Park had preached about them, and the crowds had heckled him well!"

"What was there to heckle about in that?" I asked.

"Oh, nothing particular," he answered. "The speaker was a sky pilot, and that was enough for us to jeer--"

"And now?" I asked.

"Well, I don't feel like jeering now," he answered.

I sat there and tried to picture a loving Savior knowing all, seeing all, understanding all, calling now to him, saying again, "Come, come," in spirit of all the light-hearted jeering in the past: and I left him to think about it.

Next morning I met his wife in the street, and she told me that he wanted to see me. I hurried there. He was much worse and very depressed. I suggested prayer and he was willing. Then I asked him if he was answering the Call, and he asked, "How?" I explained to him, and read the words: "all have sinned and come short of the glory of God. If we confess our sins--" and he interrupted--"I ain't no sinner, I pays twenty shillings to the pound, I ain't no drunkard either" --and I confessed to him--"I came to Jesus as a sinner: He saved me, and He will save you."

"Who told you that you were a sinner?" he asked, and I told him that the Holy Spirit convicted me and I was thankful to confess and be forgiven.

He listened, but was not convinced. "No--no-" he said, "I ain't no sinner, go and talk to that drunken woman across the road-- she's the one to be saved." And I sat on and waited.

After a time, he said very quietly: "I think you are right, Miss, but I never thought I'd have to come like that. I'll come, Miss, I'll come." And I knelt while he came and he prayed his first prayer.

He needed more help than he could get at home and more comforts for his pain-racked body, so I asked our doctor for advice, and when I suggested the Mildmay Hospital, Bethnal Green, he was glad to go. I knew he would be all right there, and he would get all the help he needed, but I did not know how transformed he would be when I saw him again. He was away for many weeks: his wife saw him on visiting days and she brought stories for all to hear of what she had seen and heard in that wonderful "house of heal-ing." "He is a changed man," she said to me. "He speaks so quietly and he's never jawed me once."

I waited to see, and one day, after many long weeks, he walked from the cab that brought him back--very really a new man.

I could scarcely believe it myself, but his greeting, "Hello, Miss," assured me it was him. He sat down on the first chair and poured out such an amazing story of what they do, and what they do not do in that wonderful hospital! The food was good, the beds were comfortable, and there was plenty of bedding--he had worn flannel all the time, he was wearing flannel then, and he touched a parcel by his side, and "that's mine, too--Matron gave it to me. But, Miss, I never saw anyone like Sister Rose: you have to do what she says, you have. One day, when I said that I could not eat my dinner, she came round, and had a good look at me and then she said: "Now, you eat your dinner' --and I ate it!" --a surprise to himself and to everybody else, except, perhaps, to Sister Rose!

He had learned a great deal about Jesus of Nazareth, and he was bent on serving Him forever. "He has been so good to me," he said, "and the ladies at that hospital--they are angels and more. They have done everything for me, and when I get back to my old pals, I'm going to tell them all about it, and my!--won't they be surprised when I tell them that there's no more swearing for me, no more pubs and drinking, and I'm going round to the Mission Service on Sunday night? We had a service in the hospital, and you should have heard us sing; yes--I am a changed man."

I went across the road to visit my first lady friend, and she beamed at me. "I am not drinking quite so much now," she said. "Me and my mates were talking about you, and we wondered why you never asked us to sign the pledge! Ain't you a teetotaller?" she asked.

I laughed. "I am a teetotaller," I answered, "but what is the good of asking you to sign the pledge? You would only do it to please me, and you couldn't keep it--besides, I know that when you get the grace of God in your heart, you won't want the drink--"

"Lor', Miss, do you mean it? she asked.

And I sat down to tell her again that Jesus saves and He keeps, and He was only waiting for her to ask Him. She sat quietly on for a bit, and then she said: "There's Mr. N------across the road: he's been ill, and he's converted and he said that I was a sinner and needing converted and I told him to mind his own business. I'm no sinner, Miss. No, Miss, that's not true--I may take a little drink and a little too much some times, but that's only fair. I'm no sinner"-- and she sniffed her disapproval of the accusation: so I sat with her for a bit, and then went back to pray more for her.

She was known all through the district as a drunkard who taught others to drink, and all the home around her had reached the lowest pitch. She swore, too, and she had a violent temper: and yet, she would not acknowledge herself to be a sinner. She was honest, she said, paid her way, looked after her family, no—she was not a sinner.

But I remembered how I had lived without Christ, unconscious of sin and my need of salvation, and He had come to me, and I told her. She was too amazed to speak, and I left her to think about it.

But one day when I was visiting at the other end of my district I seemed to hear a voice saying: "Go to Mrs. P-----, go to Mrs. P-------;" I shook myself and said I must be dreaming: but the voice was insistent, so I left the house where I was and went down the long road to find her standing at the door.

She asked me in at once, and then, moving round the table said: "I was just a-wanting of you," and fixing her bleary eyes on me: "I was a-wanting you to come." So we sat down together, and almost before I could ask, "When are you going to kneel down and ask Jesus to save you?" she answered, "Now. I was just a-wanting of you."

Together we knelt while she tried to find words to say to God, and after a while she touched me saying, "Please tell me what to say, I've never prayed before." When we got up from our knees, I put my hand on her shoulder and kissed her: she looked like a shy girl who was having her first taste of love.

I said then: "Now, Mrs. P----, you belong to Jesus, you are His forever, and no one can pluck you out of His hand." She gripped my hand and held it till it hurt. "I'm not going to tell anyone," she said. "I shall keep it to myself."

But I knew that she couldn't: she would have to tell someone: and three weeks later, as I passed down the street, I saw her daughter-in-law standing at her door. She held her baby in her arms, and she looked very depressed.

"Good-morning," I said. "Are you well?" Her answer was brief. "I've got the 'ump."

"What is the matter?" I asked. "Is your husband out of work?" She was very down, and again she answered: "I've got the 'ump, an' my husband ain't out of work." So I stood for a moment and looked hard at her, and then asked her if we could go in and sit down.

I can see the whole thing now, as it was then. Her home was one room upstairs, where she and her husband and three children lived, and she kept it clean and tidy. How she did under the circumstances, I do not know, but I did know that she paid ten shillings every week for the rent of it, and they had a hard struggle to make ends meet. She was not a drunkard: she only had a drink sometime--but to live was one long fight. Yet she took it as a matter of course.

We sat down and drew our chairs up to the table and I talked of the weather and the children, so that she could recover herself, and then I ventured, "Can you tell me what is the matter, A----? You have never spoken to me like this before": and she repeated what she had said before: "I've got the 'ump."

"Why have you got that? What is the reason?" I asked, and she blurted, "I want to be like the old gal," and I sat in silence wondering what I could say and do. I made a point of never discussing anyone in my district--what they told me was sacred, and they knew it, and so I told no one, not even her family, of the transaction that Mrs. P---had made and her commitment to God.

"She is so different," A------stated. "She never blazes now, and she has not jawed me for three weeks--and--I want to be like her."

"Do you mean to say that she doesn't lose her temper now?" I asked.

"Never," was the prompt reply. "She's quieted down, she's cleaned her place, she doesn't yell at me and ask me to get some drink for her, she's different, that's all, and I want to be like her." A----clutched at her child and wiped a tear from her eye. I saw the hunger and thirst for the Saviour, and I read to her the words from John's Gospel; "Jesus said, Ye must be born again," and she sat mute and listened. Then we prayed, and I left her in the hands of her Saviour.

She told her neighbour, and she told somebody else, and the

news spread. Those who looked on *saw* what Jesus could do, and they talked among themselves, and the Mothers' Meeting grew.

I only wish you could have heard that crowd singing. "He will hold me fast"--repeated again and again, each time louder and louder to convince themselves and everybody with them--"It is true, it is true--He *will*."

Let no one think the path was easy, for difficulties increased with the days and weeks, but the joy of the Lord was our strength in a very real way.

I learned that faith is a substance, and not the elusive thing we sometimes think it is, and I had to believe for the people in their desperate need. To see men starving and women struggling for lack of what we always have, while their children cried with hunger, made me desperate to help them, but what could I do? Mildmay did everything possible to assist the deaconesses to help their people, but the real help they needed was more than I saw. A man wanted work and he was an unskilled laborer: he went out in the morning seeking--walking miles in his search--and coming back having nothing!

I often found families like that--picture frames burnt for a bit of fire, clothing pawned to buy food: weak with hunger they struggled on, and they did not know God!

I remember one room called "home," where a family resided in their struggle for existence. They had sold all, even the mattress from their bed. The man could not get work. If I gave money to him to-day, he would need more to-morrow! What he needed and what he wanted was work, and the soles of his boots were worn through by the long tramps seeking for a job.

I sat down to face the desperate situation with them, and then I just said: "I don't know what to do, but I know Someone Who does," and they looked at me. "Why don't you call upon the Lord?" I asked. "Why don't you give yourselves to Him and let Him look after you?" The man blurted out: "I don't know anything about that. I was born and brought up in the Workhouse, and when I was twelve years of age I started out on my own. I never was trained for any work, so I have been a casual laborer all my life and I can't get work at the docks always. I wish I knew what to do." And I repeated: "Why don't you call upon the Lord? And most of all why don't you give yourselves to Him? He will look after you when you are His. He is such a wonderful Saviour and Friend. He will not fail you."

They listened, and he waved his hand round the room. "This is what I have come to."

I felt more desperate, saying I was sure that God would help them if they asked Him--so at last they knelt together and I knelt with them, and we called on the Lord in the day of trouble. Then he got up and mopping his face, looking into mine, trembling said: "He won't fail me, will He? I only want work, I can earn enough to keep us." And I assured him: "God will help you, He will not fail you"--and we knelt again to ask for a job for him the next time he went out.

I simply had to believe for them: what else could I do? And that was how I learned what faith is.

I called the next day to see how things were, to find the wife sewing at express speed. She had heard of some clothing to be made for a wholesale firm: it was something she could do, and her new faith gave her hope. She borrowed a sewing machine from a neighbor (these folk are always ready to help each other), and was hard at work, singing a song of joy. Her husband went out and he had not returned. "He must have got a job," she said, "and oh! I am so glad we asked God to help us. He answered my prayer in a half a day!" She didn't stop to talk: she was in a great hurry to finish her work, take it back and come home with money to get a meal ready for his return.

I saw it all and felt it all, and I left two tickets on the table for coal and food to tide them over the evening, and then went off to visit other homes with the same problems.

It was a wonderful life, lived as seeing Him Who is invisible. He walked the district with me, making Himself known to the people, answering their prayers, caring for their needs, and a new spirit breathed over the people. I knew that God had sent me to them, and as I listened to their stories and entered into their sorrows, I gave my heart to them and lived for them.

The deaconess dress hid the real "*me*": they saw that and recognized it, for was not Mildmay all they had ever known of help in time of need? And their trust was complete.

I can never thank Mildmay enough for all that was given me to give to the people. The cupboards are Headquarters were God's Treasure House where there was always something to give to those in need, and the deaconess in charge never wearied of giving. The careful way she looked through clothes that had belonged to someone else, and needed attention, was a lesson to all who saw it, and every deaconess was enriched to give by all she did in preparation for the people in her district. There was joy in the cupboards, and love triumphant displayed in the garments that had been sent by those who had too much and wanted to share.

True, we were sent with the Gospel of reconciliation to the people, but those at the head of affairs knew that preaching in words was not enough. If only we could make them see how He cares, and that it matters to Him when people are hungry! Did not He prove it when He fed the crowds that followed Him when He was on earth? "And seeing the multitude He had compassion on them," and He saw that they had a good meal.

The Yearly Conference at Mildmay was like going up to Jerusalem for the feast. Over a thousand gathered there for the meetings, and great preachers with a message from God were chosen to speak, and we had a week of gathering together, with the opportunity to drink deeply of His Spirit.

It was a wonderful place, filled with the Unseen Presence. There were people from all over the world, eager to be still and know. It was no ordinary crowd--there were high and low, rich and poor, and there was a message for all.

It was the year 1907, and the month of June. I left my people in the East End to join with those at Mildmay, arriving just in time for the Women's Meeting to be held at 3 p.m. on Monday afternoon. I went, of course, but my body was weary and my mind full of the sorrows of the people I had left, and I was not much inclined to listen to any speaker, especially as the one appointed was a missionary. She had been a deaconess at Mildmay before going to India, and had returned to tell us what God had done for the people among whom she lived and worked in India.

No sooner had she begun her story than I forgot tiredness and everything except that the woman on the platform was one of us. She had seen marvels unknown to us, and held her audience spell-bound, as she told of the Holy Spirit's working in the hearts and lives of Indian women converted from Hinduism. I sat up and listened. Here was the real thing. She said nothing about buildings, gave us no figures to add up: she just told of one woman, and then another, and yet another, who had been convicted of sin in their Prayer Meeting. She told how they delivered, and the joy of their salvation!

Her time was up, and she sat down, but she was recalled by the congregation. The next speaker said: "I will stand back to listen to more about India": and she did, and we heard more, until it was overtime to close the meeting.

As one of us, she brought a message for us that shook the depths of our beings, and I am glad that there are some things that cannot be shaken.

Staying in the house we saw much of her. She was different, having been across the seas and seen sights unknown to us, and having faced depths we knew nothing of: and yet there, in a city given over to idolatry, she had seen how, when the door is opened, Jesus Himself comes in and takes possession and the place is changed: an oh! How I longed to be there and see it all, but I never dreamed of going.

Every day the Conference Hall was crowded and there was a solemnity that compelled the deepest reverence all through. It was an unforgettable experience to be in the opening meeting and to stand with that vast congregation singing:

Jesus, stand among us

In Thy risen power.
Let this time of worship
Be a hallowed hour

And when we were stilled before Him we could hear His voice.

I was one in that crowd--just one--but He spoke to me there.

It was well on in the week and my thoughts were away with the people of the slums, wondering how they were and thinking of what I had seen in the district. My heart was so full of gratitude to God for saving my people, blessing them and answering their prayers, that in spirit I was telling Him that I would do anything, go anywhere for Him. "Thou art so wonderful to me," I said, "I will go anywhere." And in the silence of my heart I heard a voice softly saying: "Will you go to India?" I was so sure of the voice, and startled too, that I turned round to see who had spoken: but there was no one behind me: I was sitting in the back seat and I was trembling. The deaconess next to me put her hand on mine and asked if I felt ill.

I steadied myself to listen to the voice of the preacher; he was reading the sixth chapter of Isaiah, and Dr. Pierson knew how to read the Scriptures. They were the words of God. "Whom shall I send?" like a clarion call he read. "Who will go for us?" Then there was a long pause as if he searched for someone, and the silence was intense, and all my being hearkened for the answer, and he read: "Then said I, here am I, send me." That was all, but it lifted me out of the place I was in, right into the presence of God, and a recognition of an open door to be entered. It had never entered my head that I could be a missionary! That high a holy calling was for others fitted from their birth to be called to go, but not for me: and yet, in that meeting I was face to face with a call, and I thought I had better wait until I got back into the seclusion of my room in the Mission House in the East End--but I had no rest in my spirit.

I knew that I was not worthy: I knew that I was not prepared: I knew everything was against my going: and nothing for it except that I had heard "The Voice," and I had told Him that I would go anywhere for Him but I never dreamed of India, and the more I thought of it, the more sure I was that I was not fitted to be a missionary. "They all are born good," I said--how could I be a missionary? And I had many reasons to give why it was not for me, and yet--I was sure that I had heard The Voice that Calleth.

The end of the Conference came, and I returned to my district and to the people I loved and cared for--but, I could *not* forget.

I was called and the voice was insistent, so I told the powers that be, but no one believed me. They were all quite sure that I was in the place God meant me to be in, and I was just as sure that I was called out and I dare not disobey. Now I prepared my heart to face what it would mean, but I did not know--who does? I had no encouragement whatsoever, and every step forward was bristling with difficulties, and I felt that I could not go through with it. It would be an easy matter to pack up and go off in the urge of my spirit, but that can't be done. There are many wheels within wheels, and a Missionary Society does not send its missionaries without asking a few questions that must be answered, and that take time. I waited, because I had to wait, and nearly gave it up.

I was still reading my Bible consecutively, and that morning I was riveted by the words, "If thou refuse to go forth."

So I braced myself for the ordeal and I asked the Lord to keep me true, and one wondrous day I knew that I was accepted and would sail for India very soon. So of course, I talked about it to my friends in the slums and their remarks were interesting and full of meaning. But why I should leave them to go to "them foreign parts" puzzled them, and one man told what *he* thought, and, he added: "The Bible was in English for English people, and it had no meaning for anybody else." His wife, who was a member of the Mother's Meeting, interrupted him: "Now, Bill, you don't know what you are talking about, it says in the Bible 'Go into all the four corners of the earth and preach the Gospel,' but"--turning to me--"I don't see why you should go, you are our only friend." The seriousness of the occasion compelled a very definite plan--everyone must know, and I must know, too, just how each one stood in relation to God, and things were very definite.

Time sped by and my time was getting short. How could I leave them? They asked, and I asked myself the same question, and that could only be answered in holy communion with Him Who was sending me.

Once I wavered, and He said: "Lovest thou Me more than these?" and though I loved them dearly and they had become a part of my life, I knew He was first, and it was He Who had given them to me to take care of for Him. I could answer: "Yes, Lord, Thou knowest that I love Thee," and He claimed again His right over me. It was nearing the last day among them, and walking down the street I saw Mrs. Webb standing at her door. "Good-bye," I said, I am going soon and I am very sad because you are not saved."

She was ready with her answer. "It's like this, Miss," she said. "When I go to meeting and sit and look up, I thinks I'd like to be a Christian, I'd like to be good. Then I come home an' get me husband's tea ready, he comes home and he doesn't like that I have got ready for him and sometimes he throws it at me, and then I swears. I swears like a trooper. I'd like to be a Christian, but I can't keep it", she repeated.

So I said: "Let us go into the house and sit down," and I took my Bible from my bag. "Mrs. Webb, why don't you give your swearing to Jesus? Give yourself and your swearing to Him," and then I read: "He is able to keep that which I have committed unto Him." "He will keep you and your swearing and you will never get it back again," I said, "so swearing will not hinder you any more. No one else wants your swearing. Jesus is a wonderful Saviour and the Friend you need now."

She knew that her swearing was sin and hindered her. She knew that her language was not clean, and the blood of Jesus Christ, God's Son, cleanseth from all sin--and I sat with her and waited.

"I can't feel happy leaving you like this," I said. "Why don't you let Jesus save you?"

She stretched her hand to mine and just said, "I will." So we knelt at the little table in her kitchen and prayed. "Oh, Lord," she said, "the lidy says You can keep me from swearing, prove it to me. I want to be a Christian." Then she stopped speaking, amazed at herself, and trembling in her decision, she stood to say "Good-bye," and I left those words with her; "He is able to keep that which I have committed unto Him."

The farewell meeting in the Mission Hall was something to be remembered, and I am glad that I gave them that last meeting, for the last of the girls in my Bible Class gave herself to the Lord that night, and I left them with mixed feelings and a sore heart, for I knew their sorrows and their joys. I had entered into their struggles, making their sorrows mine—it was very difficult to leave them, and the hardest thing I ever did. It would have been impossible but for the fact that I knew in Whom I had believed, and He had called me to go with Him to seek and to save "those other sheep." He said to me: "Them also I *must* bring." So I braced myself and took it as a grand opportunity to tell them again of the love that passeth knowledge, waiting to save them, ready to keep them, and the people sang lustily: "Tell me the old, old story, of Jesus and His love," sang it as if it was all they wanted. We had no farewell hymns; we sang the Glory Song instead, and as I passed down the hall, someone started the chorus:

There'll be no dark valley when Jesus comes,
There'll be no dark valley when Jesus comes,
To gather His loved ones Home.

And it echoed down the street and all the way to the railway station on my way back to Mildmay. He calmed my mind and quieted my heart on that dark night.

Farewells and good-byes are not easy or pleasant, but they can be filled with the joy of harvest. I tested it and found it true, and that is why I write as I do.

It was as big a surprise to my family as it was too me that I should be called to be a missionary, and the remarks about it were not what a Committee would accept as a good reference. I had "done many foolish things but this surpassed them all," one member said, and "to think you are going to India! Well, that is the maddest thing to do, going to a country that was always discontented and full of unrest." "Why not go to Japan?" said another. "Or China?" said another. "Folks are natural there: besides, what good will you do?" I wondered that myself, but the fact of the call, and the opening, step by step, were so plain, that all who looked on had to admit: "It is the Lord." Even the one who told me that I "was not worth sending" confessed at the last that she must admit that "the Hand of the Lord was managing the affairs of His Kingdom." And I talked quietly with my father and knelt with him to pray, and he committed himself and all he had to the safe keeping of Him Who had waited all these years to gather him into the fold. So I held the cup of salvation and called on the Name of the Lord and I sang--yes, sang the song that He gives, that I had learned with Him through the years, and I sailed for India with my cup running over.

"If I go, I'll go with joy," I said, and I did, and the long sea voyage took none of it from me.

The glamour of the East began at Port Said, but the real thing was arriving in Bombay by night, and driving through the lamplit streets to the Mission House where we were welcomed, and the following night we began the long train journey to the United Provinces. I spent the weekend in Benares with the friend who had brought the message to Mildmay that had stirred our depths, and on Monday morning she saw me off on my last day's journey to the place where I was appointed by the Society who had accepted me, and that evening I arrived in Gorakhpur.

Nothing could have been more prosaic than the arrival in the place where God has kept me all these years. There was no romance about it: it was just the plain fact of a woman arriving and another woman meeting her and taking her home: but before I had been with her an hour, I knew that I was wanted, not only needed, and that first night was full of thanksgiving, and that is how I began my life in Gorakhpur, 36 years ago.

Faith Sees a Pathway
"By faith they passed through."-Heb.11:29.
Faith sees a pathway,
Where no man hath trod,
And walks there gaily,
Because it sees God.
O'er mountains, through valleys,
In torrents, through flood,
'Faith presses onward,
Walking with God.
Faith is a substance,
No illusive thing this,
Faith grasps God's promise,
Because it is His.
Faith sees a highway,
And walks there, serene,
Companioning always,
With the Unseen.
Faith is a conqueror,
Faith will go through,
This is God's message,
Written for you.

"Thou shalt remember that thou wast a bondman in the land of Egypt and the Lord thy God redeemed thee--" (Deut.15:15).

Redeemed" Yes--He redeemed me
He sought me and bought me
His ever to be.
His own--yes--for ever,
What else could I be
But His? --Who redeemed me
His only to be.

"Thou shalt remember all the way thy God had led thee."(Deut. 8:2)

How could I forget His wonderful guidance?
How could I help but remember His way?

His leading is triumph wrapped in obedience,
His love so compels me to trust and obey.
I do remember--remember His leading, He has been with me
all the way through;
Not once has left me, not once forsaken.

3

INDIA

I THOUGHT my book was finished there, and I laid it aside while the typing was done and I could think and pray. "Is that all?" I asked the Lord, and He reminded me that I was giving my testimony and that is not finished. And I know some will ask: "Well, was it the same when you got to India?"

Very personal questions have been put to me as to whether I found things as I expected? And was I disappointed? And did I find the promises in the Bible stand in India? Was I happy? Was I satisfied? And a thousand other questions that I cannot always answer. I began life exactly as any other missionary, with all the limitations that hem one in. After a very active life, full of movement, it is not easy to sit down and begin at the beginning of a primer to learn a language that doesn't begin with A.B.C, but it has to be done, and so I began at the beginning and started with Urdu. It looked uncommonly like shorthand, and amazing in its formation with all its characters cut into bits to form words. I was not as young as most people are, when they begin, but I knew it was the only sure way to give the message from God's Word to the people, and I was 36 years of age.

It was a lovely November day, the sun shining gloriously in a blue sky: flowering shrubs were in bloom, and I sat on the verandah gazing on the beauty into which I had come--from the fogs of London in November to the brilliant sunshine of India in November. I reveled in it, and was so cheerful about it, that the people laughed at me, saying; "You wait, you will get something else later on!" But every day began with glorious sunshine and we greeted each other with the cherry remark, "Another lovely morning," and I settled down with a Munshi to learn the language. He knew scarcely any English, which he wanted to improve, but my senior had warned me not to speak English with him but to learn Urdu from him. I need not dwell on the lower than kindergarten beginnings--the Munshi taught me in the mornings and my senior missionary helped me in the evenings, and I labored away at the weird characters to form them into words and my days were filled with study. It was a hard, stiff grind, after years of activity, and there is nothing in this climate to assist in a change of mental work; and I found it very difficult to remember what I read: but there was one lesson forced upon me as the months sped by. I thought that as the language was a real need, God would give it to me, but when I prayed for it and waited for His answer it came swift and clear; "My grace is sufficient for thee," so that I knew I must work, and anyone who knows anything about Eastern languages, knows that it is a real grind and a continual grind to learn it also as to be able to speak fluently and to understand what the people around us are saying.

After a time, I worked six hours a day then went out to visit the English-speaking people in the Railway Community, and later we started a Bible Class. We began with three, and the second week we were seven, and it grew to be an average number of forty every Tuesday. It was a marvelous opportunity for me, and we drew very near to each other in the Lord and He spoke to our hearts. From that meeting we sent our own missionary, and the love of God shed abroad in our hearts compelled us to think what love could do. We had a Prayer Meeting every Saturday morning in the bungalow opposite the Church, for those who had found the Lord and were set on doing His will. It was a very simple gathering, but of 19 memsahibs were there, 19 prayed. Their prayers were short and to the point and quite original, for they had never been to a prayer meeting before: but they launched out there, and grew in grace and liberty, and we had great times together. God was with us and prayer became a real force. Clear and definite requests were brought to the Bible Class written on scraps of paper, and when we prayed, there was no time for generalities. The air was clear, we drew nigh to God and He drew nigh to us, and the Holy Spirit guided us to pray the prayers that it was the will of the Father to grant, and we watched for the answers.

That Bible Class is a holy, happy memory. The members are scattered far apart now. Those who are on earth still carry on in the countries where they dwell, but many have passed into the Father's House and they found their way there while they lived in Gorakhpur.

There was no language school in those days. It was a solitary grind sitting at a table, books piled around, and a Munshi listening to the sound made by the ardent missionary who was living for the day when she could go out and tell the people in a language they understood that God had called them to repentance. It was a painstaking way and the movements were slow and often monotonous: there was nothing easy about it, but I am glad now, that I found it so difficult to learn and to remember what I read. Some people find it easy, but not many. I know there are unmentioned, yet very precious, lessons learned with the study, and they compel attention, for East is East and West is West, and it is a very searching experience to be where all things are new and everybody is a stranger and the language spoken the strangest of all. There is no romance about it, life is real, life is earnest, and it takes all there is of a man or woman to get down to it and get through: and there are no short cuts to the goal, but it is all worthwhile. I worked hard, and the promise the Lord Jesus made to His disciples held good for me. "I am with you all the days," He said, and He disciplined me into real application to the work in hand, and there was to be no shirking. Language study is no sinecure, for examinations are to be passed in a given time, and, as I said before, I was not young; but I made no excuses for myself, I worked and prayed, and worked, and the first examination was passed and I began another language--this time Hindi, and the characters that form the written part are a quite different, and not so complicated.

In the city we have elementary schools, mostly for Hindu girls, and this is their language, so I went to school and sat on a stool like a teacher, listening to the children, picking up sounds and learning expressions. At home I had a Pundit to teach me; but I learned the simple form of speech from the children, beginning in the lowest class and little by little I arrived at the top, and could ask questions and read Bible stories which they requested of me in their own words. I learned much more there than anywhere else. None could speak English, I had to know their language to speak to them, and I was much too curious to be content with anything less than understanding what they said. My interest grew in the schools, and I was invited to the homes of the children, and when my Hindi examination was passed, I began to teach in their Zenanas.

It was a wonderful experience to be taken there, and I was gripped by the appalling apathy. No one seemed to say "Come and help us." The women were curious and asked very personal questions as if nothing were private in life, and I answered as many as I could, but held to my purpose that if I listened to them, they must listen to me. And their reading books were opened and the Bible woman with me gave the lesson which was the slowest thing I have ever seen, and there was always the Scripture lesson with questions and answers and all the time a prayer in my heart: "Lord what wilt Thou have me to do?" It all felt so barren, so lifeless, and the atmosphere thick with superstition, and in some houses Satanic forces seemed to rule supreme. We went into windowless rooms, where light only came in through the door, sat on the edge of their beds where there were no chairs, and gave lessons to women who had never been to school and wanted to learn to read. We made friends with them, learned from them, and tried to picture what it must be never to go out for a walk, never to step out into the street, always, all the days, every day, to live in seclusion and never once to go out to a meeting. I asked, "Why?" and the answer was one word, "Custom." I asked other questions and most of them had the same answer: "It is not our custom"-- and they settle down in it and never attempt to move out of it, for they are bound by custom, and customs do not easily change in the East. But--we can and do go to them, and sometimes lethargy is stirred and a glimmer of light beyond their dwelling-place reaches them, and something awakens in them and the scene is changed.

The interest grew as I got to know more, and my heart opened to the women who suffer in seclusion. I began to think how I could tell these people what Jesus could do for them, and I went deeper into the language. Oh! to be simple enough to be able to tell these people so clearly that they would not think about me, but see and hear Him.

I had still another exam to pass, and I was studying to become proficient in Urdu while I did a full day's work in the Zenanas and schools. To see the people and talk with them was a great incentive to speak their language as they did. That winter we went into camp and lived among the people in the villages, and again another world opened out before me. We live on the border of Nepal, and see the snows on a clear day, but here in camp we had a close-up view. Never had I seen anything so wonderful as those high peaks of everlasting snow--deep blue lower hills stood between us and them--and they are called Nepal--he closed and forbidden land!--- where no Christian may live and no missionary may go: but the people come down and we see them, and talk with them and they with us. Miles of yellow mustard fields dotted with the white poppy patches that produce opium--and palm trees near and far, standing with other trees in groups among the villages, from the scene before us--I was entranced by it all. But the need of the people was just the same as it was in Gorakhpur--malaria was rampant and nearly every grown-up person had a goiter: some were nearly the size of a small football. They were 40 miles from a doctor and had never seen one: there they lived and suffered, and there was no one there to help them, and they had never heard the name of Jesus! They knew nothing about the way of salvation—God sent me there with my senior missionary, and we went out every morning to have meetings in the villages, and the people flocked to our camp every evening to tell us their troubles and to ask help for their sicknesses.

We stood before the highest snow peaks in the world while the sunset clothed them with gold, and Nepal was turned into deep purple hue, and the people had not even noticed it! Their sorrows, their aches, their pains, and their struggles for existence had claimed all their attention. What could we do in the face of such need? We were neither doctors nor nurses, but we could do something, and suffering does make all the world akin. So we opened a little medicine chest that was given to me when I was leaving England, and we studied the book inside it and sought help from Him Who sent us, and then listened again to the people who suffered. We gave what help we could in the Name of Jesus, and He was true to His Word and healed many who came. But the destitution was appalling and we saw what real need is—we lived among those people for four months, and then we returned to Gorakhpur and the work—but we had glimpses of possibilities, and longings were created in us for people with gifts of healing, men and women on fire for God who would go in and out to preach the Gospel of our Lord Jesus Christ and gather the lost ones home. The need is beyond my telling and there are few there to meet it. Sometimes I seem to hear again the voice that spoke to me in Mildmay; "Whom shall I send? Who will go for us?" and it may be that some who read this will say: "Here am I, send me." If you come and if you let God rule your life and guide you in all your doings, if you never lower your standards, and never compromise, you will experience the truth of those words: "They that do know their God shall be strong and do exploits."

India is waiting for someone who is not afraid to show love in all its practical reality--India wants sympathy that is healthy and fearless--India is looking for someone who can show them what Jesus is like. "We have heard a great deal about salvation," said one to me, "*now* we want to see it." Who will come and show them. There are millions in this district alone who have never heard--will no one come to tell them? I knelt with Preetee on Sunday morning after a talk about our high and holy calling and she prayed to understand what it all meant. She was a convert from a Brahman caste, and she had left all to follow the Lamb, and was going about with me to tell others of the wonderful Saviour she had found.

We met two widows who had been to Khatmandu seeking salvation--"God dwells there," they said. "We saw the mountains He made and we went to get a vision of Him"--and Preetee was swift to answer: "I, the Holy One, dwell with him who is of a lowly heart and of a contrite spirit," and she explained the way of salvation to them. They stood in awe and looked towards the everlasting snows and then moved on and we came in to pray. Preetee was troubled: she had begun to feel that the day was far spent for her, and as we prayed she revealed her heart's deep longings. "I am coming soon," she said, "coming soon to thee and my hands are empty" --she stretched them out--"see, they are empty! Must I go into Thy presence empty-handed? No. No. I cannot." Her voice trembled as she pleaded for them to be filled with treasures she could take with her there--and we wept together--wept with longing, and ask the Lord of the Harvest to water the seed we were sowing and give us a harvest to bring in to Him. I returned to Gorakhpur, and it was time for my final examination. I did not feel ready--who does? The people and their need had gripped me and the difficulties compelled me to search my heart for a solution, but I realized that whether I was ready or not, that examination must be taken and I must face the result.

So, from that heartbreaking need I sat down to prepare as much as I could with the help of the High School Master, and when the day arrived, I sat down with papers filled with questions and a feeling of utter inability to answer them, and a brain that seemed to belong to somebody else. It was the final test--the last and the most difficult papers--and the one in the room to supervise said: "You had better read them through," and she gave me a time limit.

Two days of writing, answering questions and translating, then the papers were sent off, and I returned to the city with its clamoring need. A month later a letter came from the powers that be saying that I had passed the written examination, and now must go to Allahabad for the oral. Of all things that touch every nerve in your body, there is nothing quite so bad as a language oral examination. The journey there takes twelve hours in the train, and then the meeting with other candidates may cause one to forget some of one's fear, but it is a nervous party that sits round the dinner table, and discusses the weather and the stations, and never a word about the examination, until some brave person asks the time we must start on the morrow. There's plenty of kindness and encouragement given by the Seniors we are staying with, but nothing seems to stop the cold water trickling down the back, and nothing stills the trembling within--why it should be so, I don't know, for no one could be kinder than the examiners--and yet--we who go to face them trust more to our memories than to them, and then a question is put--simple, easy, well-known--but the answer? They know it perfectly well: they are great men who have spent twenty, thirty, and forty years teaching and preaching in the language they are patiently waiting for simple folk like me to answer--and after a pause the question is repeated and the answer is there--so the examination begins.

Think of men with their knowledge patiently listening to the stammering out of words by missionaries of two or three years' standing. The amazing thing is that they seem to have power to draw words from you that you didn't know were there, and you go from one subject to another looking carefully at the paper, gaining courage as you go, until a real conversation begins, and then, hey presto!--for a Hindu or a Moslem has been called in to carry on a conversation and has spent some time teaching the language to missionaries, and yet--has not sought the Lord: here's a chance, and there's no more halting. Why is he still a Hindu or Moslem? He has read the Scriptures with his pupils; does he not think they are true? He is sure they are, and somehow then the conversation grows, the fire burns, examination is forgotten, here is a man to be saved, what is hindering him? All eagerness to cause him to know that God so loved him that He gave His only begotten Son to live and die for him--did he not know this truth? Did he not believe it? And before we had finished time was up. The great men had made their notes: there was one more subject not quite so fluently discussed and then it is all over, and we stand to say farewell. It was like the finish up of a party with its genial leave-takings, and yet--it is one of the most momentous occasions in any missionary's life-- and it was so in mine. The goodbyes and handshakes, the smiles and good wishes, then the door is opened and I step out freer than I have ever been before, for that phase of my life was over--I could go out to tell the story.

"Did you pass?" asked my senior when I got back, "did they say anything to you?" And then there comes another phase and hopes begin to quiver, assurance is nil, and then kindness has reached its zenith, there's a voice calling for attention, someone runs to see, and a telegram is handed in and my name is on the envelope.

"You have passed. Congratulations," is all it said, but it turned our evening into hilarity, for the great people had taken the trouble to let me know that it was over and I had passed all the language examinations.

Why do I tell all this? you may ask, and I say: "I want to encourage you who have waited through this war and the years had added to your age: and it may be that someone will say: 'It is too late, you can't go now, you are too old. You will have to stay where you are, you can't learn the language at your age'". Don't believe them: if you are called--obey--and God will see you through. God never called anyone to an easy life--His paths are all cross-marked. Things may be a little more difficult because you are not as young as you were, but nothing is impossible to him or her that believeth--the years have given you an experience that will help you in the future; the patient waiting has added strength to your character and steadied your going out and your coming in--and application is not as flimsy as it was--and above all and through all, the voice is saying to you: "Blessed are they that wait for Him. You couldn't come before, you can come now."

The examinations over, there was a freedom in the air that was never there before, and I stepped out in liberty--not that I had learned all there was to learn--oh, no--I very soon found that the past was the beginning, and there's nothing like daily work among the people where no English is heard or spoken to help to fix in the mind what little knowledge there is, and I was free to learn and to go on learning and oh, how I wanted to do the real thing. So I was appointed to a certain district and I began in real earnest. "This is *mine,* I am responsible to God for it," I said to myself, and I went into Zenanas and began to teach the women to read and write, and to give a lesson from the Bible. A teacher was with me to do the needful and I helped as I could; and I discovered that language spoken as they speak it does not come in the night or even by thinking--it was very elusive. I came back to work and to search out meanings of words and to go out again to try to give out what I learned, and the joy of doing what I came out to do was always there.

The cold weather was over and the hot weather began, and there was nothing in the air to exhilarate our goings out, and yet it is taken for granted that we continue, nothing daunted, hot or cold. Teachers gather for prayer, the conveyance is ready, and we go off to airless houses, down smelly gullies, where every smell is a kingdom in itself, to see women who never leave their houses and to tell them what God has prepared for them that love Him. There are always more than the pupil there, and by the time the lesson has been given there is always a company waiting to be told something that is written in the Book we carry about with us. There is a great interest in this bit of work, for no one sits quietly to listen while the teacher says all she has prepared to say. The interruptions are legion--"How old are you?" was one of the first questions put to me! "Are you married?" "Not married! What have your parents been doing not to get you married?"

They are quieted for a bit, and the Bible story proceeds and everybody looks interested and a voice from the back asks the question: "How much did you give for that dress material?" and those in front come close to feel its worth--only the simplest cotton material, but they are interested and must have an answer. They have this one break in the week and they made the most of it in their own way, and we want to teach them of the highest and the Best, but there is nothing straightforward, and the daily round of Zenanas is like seeking for some precious pearl: "Where is it? oh, where is it"? And we go on undaunted by any interruption, and then sometimes there is a light in the eye of one who has listened and heard, and she draws a little closer, and I remember the day when a Hindu widow whispered: "How did you know about me?" I looked at her and said: "The Lord Jesus is seeking for you and He sent me to find you." It was joy unspeakable and full of glory to me, for not one of those we go to have the privileges you have, and they would never hear the story of Jesus and His love if no one went to tell them.

The schools are the most primitive anyone could imagine: there is no equipment, no desks, no bookcase or library. An ordinary house is rented, some cheap matting procured, a *dai* is engaged to call the children, and a teacher sallies forth to teach. We have prepared some wooden slates painted black, and purchased some white chalk in the bazaar, and the children come and squat on the floor and begin their first lesson. A blackboard stands against the wall, the teacher produces some paper-backed books, and every child is eager to possess one, but there are not enough to go round, and they cost money. So the preliminaries are over, the words of a *bhajan* (Hindustani hymn) are taught. They learn to clasp their hands together and to close their eyes, while the teacher prays, and more children saunter in after a time. There is much coming and going: they have not learned what regularity is or the necessity of continual application to learn to read and write. They simply want to read, and some children are a long time before they come daily. I went in search of some to ask why they were absent, and the mother just said: "She didn't want to go yesterday and today, she will go tomorrow if she wants to." Bit by bit the teacher makes the lesson so attractive that a child goes not because she is sent, or is compelled, but just because she feels like it—she wants to. And so, we are ready for them when they come, and marvelous to relate, the school is soon filled, classes are formed, more teachers are added, once in the year there is an examination.

We have four such schools, and they go up to the 7 Standard, and the children pass out when they are about eleven or twelve years of age, because they are married and must go to live in distant villages where their husbands have waited for them since they were little children. They can read the Bible and write a letter, and most of them can knit and sew, and they go off into the unknown to scatter the seed sown in their hearts while they learned in the Zenana School. They have learned to pray and have their own prayer meetings in the school. They know the Scriptures and sing songs of Zion—who can tell the end? Who knows what difference it has made to the community to which they belong? Thousands have passed through our schools since I came here, and they still go on, a light in a dark place, and love unmeasured, poured out by every teacher is still flowing. They are simple women, not highly educated, but they can teach what they know. "Not many mighty, not many noble are called, but God hath chosen the weak things, the base things of the world, and things that are despised too, that no flesh should glory in His presence." And He gives them grace to go on. They are God's chosen—sent forth to witness to the children in a non-Christian city, and the children carry the message to their parents, and we know that what is of God will last forever.

There were the schools, there were the Zenanas, and there were the villages in the cold weather, and for five and a half years I was there, telling the old, old story, giving out messages, teaching and preaching, and there was not much to see for it all. It had been a long night, and the morning seemed a long way off. The climate was exhausting, the people were diffident, and I felt numb as I looked at things as they were. "Why don't people come out?" I asked. "Why does no one openly confess that they are on the Lord's side?" And every Teacher and Bible-woman working with us gave the same answer; "We are sowing the seed: the people listen well now, we are only sowers." "Is there to be no harvest?" I questioned. "Wait and see," was their answer, but it did not satisfy me. "If the men in your village sow seed in their fields, do they expect a harvest?" I asked. "Of course they do," was their chorus. "Then we must expect too"--and they looked at me wondering. But I held to it that whatever a man sows, he reaps *that*-- and yet--I saw no harvest. What was the good of it all?

I never worked so hard in my life as I did those five and a half years. What was amiss? Why didn't I see at least the wheat ripening in the fields? I looked at the English community--I had a harvest here: but among the Indians in the city and villages where I had toiled unceasingly there was so little to see for it. I made friends with the women in Zenanas, and was welcomed in the villages. The schools had increased in numbers. "We are sowers" said the Teachers. Yes, we were. "Is that all?" I asked, and faced the thought of meeting the Lord of the Harvest. What could I say to Him: As far as I knew I had been faithful, had done what I could, and among other things had gone with two Bible-women across the border into Nepal and given the message to the people in the village across the border. It was thrilling but it was not satisfying.

I looked around. There was so little to see for all that labour, and then my eyes rested on a little child. She had been brought to me when a tiny baby she looked like a skeleton when she arrived, as if her wee body would drop to pieces. I took her in my arms and held her up to Jesus, and then I sat down and prayed: "Gentle Jesus, meek and mild, look upon this little child, and oh! Teach me how to bring her to Thee." That was three years before. She was a happy little girl, loved and cared for by the young officers in the Salvation Army. I was not allowed to have her here: we had no place for children in our compound, and I had no one to take care of her. These friends added to their service by doing this for me. She was brought in to see me, and I went over to see her as often as I could, so we knew each other, and I left her in their care. There was very little else that I could see, but there were several in the Zenanas who believed in Jesus, and I left them to find for themselves the wonderful pathway of prayer, reminding them that Jesus said: "Whatsoever ye shall ask the Father in My Name, he will do it." They were my last days with them, and my last words to them, and I said, "Good-bye" to their call, "Come back soon" but I hoped that God had something better than that for me: and it was wrapped in a special wish that I might not return to Gorakhpur.

It was the spring of 1914 when I returned to Mildmay. The atmosphere of the place refreshed all my being. I went about speaking at meetings, attended Keswick Convention and stayed with fellow missionaries drinking deeply of the Spirit in his fullness there. It was wonderful to sit in that crowd and listen to men sent of God to tell us a more excellent way, and I sang with the crowd, "Like a river glorious, is God's perfect peace." Is there anywhere else on earth where it is sung with such blessed assurance? I prayed with the multitude and talked with those who wanted to go further on with God, and I made no secret of not wanting to go back to Gorakhpur, but one evening I was arrested. Rev. Stuart Holden was speaking about the three men who were standing before the king; "We know our God, Whom we serve, is able to deliver us, but if not--we shall obey Him just the same: we will not serve thy gods" (See Daniel 3:16,17,18). Then the Lord spoke through Mr. Stuart Holden: You have come to Keswick disappointed because of the way--you have trusted the Lord to do some great thing and there is a blank--you have prayed for a revival, and nothing has happened--and you are thinking: "The God Whom we serve is able--but--but--but if not?"--what is your answer?".

I sat there, one in a congregation of three thousand people, and I knew God was speaking to me. My years in Gorakhpur were like a moving picture before me: scene after scene passed by: I did not want to go back there: I wanted to try another place where, perhaps, I should be more successful. "Will you go back to the old life? You have prayed for revival. Our God Whom we serve is able-- but if not"--the silence was intense--and he waited as a man knows how to wait with a message straight from God. "But if not--" he repeated--I laid my choice in the dust, and knelt at the Cross to pray anew: "Create in me a clean heart and renew a right spirit within me," and I went out to sit by the river to renew my covenant with God. I was willing to go back any time, even now, and before I left Keswick a letter reached me from my Senior missionary. She was in despair, she said, the Mission wrote of closing the Station. I went back to London and asked to be sent back. "What about deputation?" was the question put to me. I still pleaded to be sent back as soon as possible. The war broke out, and the way seemed to close--but the Lord had found His willing slave. I had found treasures even in Keswick; one is with me here. He sent me back after seven months' furlough to be and to do His good pleasure.

I somehow expected to find things different, but as I crossed the Kacherry ground on the way to church the bricks were in the same place, the people I met were just the same, and when I got back to the city there was no change in the atmosphere. "But if not" rang in my spirit, and I called a halt. "What is it, Lord?" I asked. "Where can I find the sheep that is lost?" And He answered: "Ask of Me and I will give thee the heathen for thine inheritance." "Ask of Me." It took some time for me to grasp that I needed to give more time for asking in prayer: and as I thought, I realized that I must rise early to pray--there are no interruptions then, the world is quiet and still--but how could I do it, with the question. The climate encourages sleep.

Anyhow, I could try it, and I did--but when I knelt I went to sleep again. I tried again, with the same result. I opened my Bible to read, but my mind was not awake: I was a dazed early riser who could sleep better than pray, and I was so unsuccessful that I dropped it to face things in the day, and to put the question that must be answered—"Why did I get up early? What was the good of it? and Why? Why? Why? Such strange endeavor to get up before the dawn? I questioned myself, and it sifted down to this answer: "I was really getting up to meet Him." If I say I am getting up to have a quiet time, it doesn't convey much to me, but to put it into plain bald truth—"I want to meet Him," all my being responds, difficulties melt away. I am awake and glad and free and eager to get down before Him. I can arise and go to my Father, and I don't want to stay in bed.

It was a wonderful revelation to me, and when I got up He was there to meet me, and He taught me how to pray, and how to wait before Him. The Scriptures opened out priceless treasures, and I soon learned that real prayer is vital in its working, and it wasn't long before I discovered that it takes time to know God. "Be still and know" became a reality. I could not live on the past, I must go ahead but I needed guidance, and how could He guide me if I would not wait for it? Very soon I could say with the Psalmist: "He waketh me morning by morning," and I acquired the habit of rising at 4 o'clock to watch and pray and to hear what He would say to me in His Word. It was then that prayer became fundamental and the power in work. Prayer changes things, and it changes people too, and all my life has been transfigured by the habit of prayer cultivated, persevered and pursued. It is a wonderful way of getting to know God: real prayer leads to real communion and a growing fellowship with Him with Whom we have to do. The place of prayer increases in holiness and the Shekinah Glory is there and an understanding of the words to Moses: "Take off thy shoes from off thy feet, for the place whereon thou standest is holy ground." It is there He calms my mind and makes quiet my heart, and then He speaks to me and my soul doth magnify the Lord, for He has done great things for me.

We gathered the Teachers and Bible women together to search

the Scriptures and we discovered the way of blessing in Malachi 3: "Bring all the tithes into the store house and prove Me, saith the Lord." So we sat down before Him and talked with Him: we all wanted the way of blessing, and this was the start off. In those days a Teacher had ten rupees a month--one rupee is a tenth, and tithing required much careful thought. But the words were clear and direct --"Bring *all the tithes*... and prove Me ...saith the Lord"--and those dear, old-fashioned Indian Christian women sat counting the cost. Would they? Could they? How? There was never any surplus when all was paid, and one rupee less was a great deal, yet God said: "Bring *all* the tithes," and so--. We talked all round it: we did not want to evade it, neither did we want to miss the blessings, and there was some puzzling as to how they would manage if they did it. So I suggested that they try it for one year and if they found they could not manage without that rupee, or whatever it was, they could give it up. There was a glad eagerness to try and see, which is to do exactly as it is written: "Prove Me, saith the Lord, and see if I will not open the windows of heaven and pour you out such a blessing as you shall not have room to receive it." After that there was no hesitation and we all began in real earnest. The amazing thing was that the air seemed clear and we saw where we were going.

I was glad that I had come back to them and they were more bent than ever on sowing the seed which is the Word of God. The one little child came often to see me and they all loved her. "She is Shanti (Peace), they said. "God will give us more": and we went on our way rejoicing. In those days there were seeds sown that live to-day. We have one here to whom I was talking to-day. She was a little girl then, and wandered freely in our Compound with her father who was tending the cows. If she saw me anywhere in the bungalow she ran in to be with me and to chatter about all she could think of to keep me company. I had no thought of her coming to stay, but I told her one day about the little girl who was ill and the Lord Jesus went to see her and he made her well. She listened quietly and went away remembering, and sometime after she asked: "Is that gentleman who went to see the little girl when she was ill a relative of yours?" I couldn't remember talking to the child about a gentleman, but she enlightened me. "You know you said she was as big as I am and He made her well. Was He a doctor? Was He a relation of yours? I told my mother and father and they said He was." Then I remembered, and I told her a bit more about the Saviour Who loved her and wanted to save her. "He is God's Only Son and He told me to come to India to tell little girls like you that He is the Giver of Salvation and He is always calling people saying: 'Come unto Me, and I will give you rest." You must tell your mother and father about Him," and she ran off saying she would. She often came and played around while I worked, and sometimes we had a talk about Jesus, and she always asked me to tell her more about the Kind Gentleman Who loved little girls, and I prayed she might know Him. She was a Hindu, born in a Hindu home, and before she was 12 years old she went off to a far distant village to live with her husband, and we heard no more of her for years. Suddenly, one day she appeared when we had moved into the new bungalow. She stood on the verandah, eyes flashing, and a broad grin, and picking up the punkah rope she began to pull. After a time her tongue was unloosed and a torrent of words poured forth. She was so glad to be here--she wanted to come to see how we fared. She had walked all the way--she could stay ten days--she would pull the punkah every day, and then walk back. A little chuckle, and then she repeated: "I can stay ten days. I think much about the Kind Gentleman Who loved little girls like me, but I don't remember His Name" and she chattered away to the two women engaged for the work, and asked if they knew what she had heard those years ago? Then the conversation began in real earnest, and her descriptions were given with signs and vividly told, and my verandah lost its quietude. She came and learned a little more, and went back to tell the folk in her village. Everybody liked her, she had such a good tempered, happy nature, and was willing to do anything to help anyone. So she was very popular. The temperature was 117 in the shade and more than that where she sat pulling the punkah. She mopped her face and laughed, and I told her to let the women do the work they were paid for. She just laughed and tossed her head, saying: "They don't love as I do," and they laughed with her. They were simple village women engaged every hot spell to come to pull the punkah, for which they received their wages--and Pyari was content.

She went back to her village, and for two years or more we heard nothing of her: then in the beginning of the cold weather she appeared again and we did not know her.

All the shine had gone from her, her body had shrunken, she was gaunt and thin, and no smile greeted us. "I want to stay," she panted. "I have walked all the way, my heart is broken, and I am too sad to live." We opened the door and she walked in, sat down and gave herself up to grief. Old Bua took her in, and she settled down as if she meant to stay. She chose her own work--she wanted to wash all the crockery and pots and pans--and she did it in real earnest. Everything was made spotlessly clean and she was quiet and industrious. There was no thought of going back in her mind, her heart was fixed, and she applied herself to doing all she could. Weeks and months passed by while she went into school and learned to read, attended the Bible classes and was always at family prayers. She was drinking in the Truth and learning to know her need, till one day she asked to be baptized. I took her into my room and told her something of what it meant. She listened very quietly, and then said: "I would give myself to Him but I don't know how."

In the simplest form of speech I reminded her of how she came to me. "Yes, yes," she replied. "I always wanted to come to you, but I couldn't stay. Then when my heart was broken I came and you received me." "Did all of you come, or did you leave your heart in the village?" I asked. "No, no, all of me came. I was very sad, and my heart was broken. I was in great need and had only one sari which I wore when I arrived and I had no bedding." "And did I ask you many questions?" "Not one. You looked at me in love and never said a word and I came right into the compound. And then--I was in and I stayed." "And that is how you come to Jesus and give yourself to Him."

She brightened up and was eager to give herself. We knelt in prayer while she poured out all her longings to Him Who had called her, and then she went back to her washing up.

Six weeks later, she was baptized in the name of the Father and of the Son and of the Holy Ghost, and radiant smiles came back to stay.

"I am like you now, I am inside. I had a dream and the Lord Jesus told me so," she said confidentially one morning. I was puzzled and asked what she meant, and this was her dream;

"I was asleep when a beautiful white light came into my room and I sat up to see what it was. Then I heard a voice and peering to see, I saw the figure of a man wearing white robes. I was afraid to move till the voice spoke again. He called me by my name, He said that I belonged to His family. I cried out: 'How? How can that be?' And He bent over me and whispered: 'You have been baptized into the family of God,' and I asked: 'Like Mamaji?' 'Yes, like Mamaji,' He answered, I laughed and knelt where He was. I am satisfied now: I am like you: I came to Jesus and He took me in," and she laughed for joy of heart. She is so simple, she just trusts. I was talking to her again to-day, for she has stayed with us through the years. Now she has changed her work from washing up pots and pans, and has a passion for sweeping and cleaning the floors. She is happy doing that any time of the day, and when I told her that heaven is paved with gold, she stood with eyes wide opened and gesticulated with her hands, and then remarked: *"Kaise khubsurat* (how beautiful)!"

"You will have lots to do there," I said.

"Would you like to polish the floors?" Her joyous answer was a clear understanding of that wonderful land that is fairer than day. She polishes the floor and talks about what it will be like to be there. I heard her telling a little girl that those who have washed their robes in the Blood of the Lamb will stand near the Throne and sing the hymn we learn here! She belongs to those simple folk who know how to trust and not be afraid--she learns, but she never grows clever. She goes out to the village dispensary to give her testimony and to tell the people there how Jesus found her, and there is not a dull hearer. She is vivid in her descriptions. She can read her Bible, and her prayers are a revelation of love and care for others--her simplicity lasts and never wears out--she is one of those rare jewels found unexpectedly and treasured for their worth. The years of her pilgrimage are fast going and she is happy because she knows where she is going, and I often think of the joy she will get when she finds herself at home in the Father's House to stay for ever and ever.

I am thinking back to those first years in Gorakhpur that I had spent sowing the seed, and because I had not seen the harvest, I hoped never to see the field again. She was only a little Hindu girl, who played around our Bungalow and when she came in to see me, I told her about Jesus and read stories from the New Testament to her. Well," the seed is the Word of God." I was a sower and the seed fell into her heart, which was good ground. I left it, and forgot that it takes time to germinate. The Lord of the Harvest was watching over His Word to perform it, and because it did not come as quickly as I expected it, I was disappointed and left it, and did not even remember it when I got to England: but God is Love, and He arrested me, and after he had spoken to me I was willing and ready to come back. Supposing I had chosen my own way and place to live and work in? Where should I be now? I can never thank Him enough for His patience with me in my self-will and for saving me from it, and bringing me back, saying: "Thy servant is ready and willing to do what *Thou* shalt appoint."

I had no idea of the harvest I have seen: I never dreamed there was such abundance of fruit that remaineth, and it with us still. I look up and through the window: I see splashes of scarlet: it is only two little girls, and near them is a boy holding the branch of a tree so that they can get the leaves: ripples of laughter come through the flower-scented air. They are playing in the garden: they have lately come back to me. They have been living in the closed land, for their father belongs to Nepal: and no one is allowed to confess Christ there. He was in India, and he went back because it is easier for a man to get rich there, and he gathered must spoil: he was increased in goods, but his soul was starved. His children lost all the Christian disciple they needed, and in despair he cried unto the Lord. In humility and conviction of his sin his heart said: "I will arise and go to my Father and will say unto Him: 'Father, I have sinned against heaven and before Thee, and am no more worthy to be called Thy Son,'": and oh! How he longed for someone to help him--and just there as he stood-almost too miserable to live, the postman arrived with a big envelope and addressed to him, and it contained a beautiful photograph of him with his family taken long ago and coloured to make it real and kept as a sacred treasure by one who knew him then.

A short letter dropped on the ground while he gazed on the speaking picture that told him what he was, and he stooped to pick up the letter. It was written after much prayer, and the urge of the Spirit sent it off to plead with him to return to the Lord, to seek the old paths. He was so overcome that He brooked no delay, and after five years in the far country he came home to his Father and said unto Him: "I am not worthy to be called Thy son, but oh! I will do anything if only thou wilt take me back." I heard him pray his prayer and saw his brokenness and depression. In his eagerness to come back he left all--houses, land, cattle, and money lent out on usury--and there he stood with his family. He also left a good-paying job, for he was a teacher by profession, and he stood facing a blank future with a wife and family. But he had come back to his Father, and I reminded him that God would show him what to do. So we all knelt together to pray for guidance, and the following night he left us to go to a far distant city to find work so that he might be able to earn his living to support his family and begin life anew.

The mother of a lovely girl of 12 and the boy of 14 was the first baby I had, the one bit of harvest I could see in the first 5 1/2 years here. She was the first fruits, and when she grew up she was married to this young man who was a real Christian, and they went off together to the Theological Training School, and passed with honours. Their next step was to a far distant city among the hills to work among the people there. She visited the homes and taught the women and helped many into the Kingdom: he taught in the school and helped in the villages. They talked about ordination since he had a gift for preaching. He was loved and respected by the people and the missionaries made much of him. They wrote regularly. They were settled. They had two children and they asked Bua to stay with them. She went the three days' journey and thoroughly enjoyed her stay, and the end was crowned by a visit from the Viceroy. This gave a great glory to Bua's visit, but she could not get over her surprise at the Viceroy being dressed like any other man—just ordinary clothes, no crown on his head, no gold braid on his coat, and his trousers (she remarked) were just like those the men there wore—"and," she added, "I stayed two days to see him!" I think she was disappointed, for she expected to see the glory of the highest in the land, and he came as a man to see men and to encourage those who were doing good.

Bua came back to us and told the story to the family, and she stood high in their estimation. She belonged to them: she had stood quite near to the place where the Viceroy of India passed, and they felt the honour of almost having touched him, and appropriated it to themselves. They strutted off with pride and talked to each other about it. Our young folk wrote to us and told us their version. All that could be seen in that brief visit drew the interest of that man in power and the people wrote of it as a never-to-be-forgotten visit. They were cheered and helped and encouraged: he had spoken to the missionaries as man to man, understanding their problems and difficulties. He was the Viceroy of India, he was also a man—and that was what Bua saw, though she puzzled and still puzzles about the lack of regal garments when he paid a brief visit to the village where she was staying.

FRUIT

FRUIT

A TRUE WITNESS
"Called to be . . . a Witness."
A true witness delivereth souls."--Prov. 14:25
Lord, make me that, Yes Lord, just that,
A witness true to thee,
Delivering souls from sin and death,
Wherever I may be.
A witness Lord, filled with Thy love,
Stretching a hand to save,
What'er the cost, to find the lost,
Remembering--Jesus gave.
A life poured out; unstinted love,
Would I pour out for Thee,
To be a witness, delivering souls,
Oh, Saviour Lord, make me.

ꕥ 2 ꕥ

WITNESS

I T WAS NOT easy to get reconciled to the fact that a community was called "Christian" whether they had been born again or not. They were not Hindu, they were not Mohammedan, they were called Christian--and the question, is he or she a Christian? did not convey the vital meaning associated with it in the Homeland.

A friend with years of experience in this land advised me not to ask such questions. "It isn't done," she said, and I puzzled a good bit about it. But was slow to learn. We were in great need of Bible women and Teachers to go to the Zenanas: we wrote to friends far and near for help and they answered, "We also want the kind you write of, but we cannot get them," and then I asked myself, "What would Jesus do?" It sent me to the Book, and the answer stood out before me: "He ordained twelve that they might be with Him." It was as if some new light had fallen on Holy Writ. We generally speak of ordination after long training in college, and the "Powers that be" know for certain that the candidate is called to the ministry: but Jesus ordained the twelve that they should be with Him, and it gave me much food for reflection.

The wonder of it thrilled my soul! Ordained to be with Him--not ordained after you have been with Him--and I began to think of the details it meant in each life.

Slowly the fact became clear that what Jesus wants is that we should be with Him, so that His life of pure holiness should be to us the most natural thing in the world.

The very fact of being with Him sweeps away many problems that would baffle and hinder the upward way. To talk with Him, walk with Him, learn to do the will of God, see how He lives, hear how He speaks, for never man spake like This Man--to--be--with--Him, all the time!

I turned the pages of the Sacred Book to read, mark, learn, and inwardly digest the fact, and then I read: "And, that He might send them forth to preach, *and* to have power to heal sicknesses *and* to cast out devils." Ordained to be with Him and then to be sent. It was that little important word *"and"* that riveted me. If ever there was a need for the same directions it is *now*.

The record of Him is summed up in one short sentence: "He went about doing good and healing all who were oppressed with the devil." Those chosen men saw it all, and one of them wrote it down that we might know. Then there was a day when Jesus very quietly said to those who were with Him: "I have ordained you that you should go, and that you should bear much fruit." Ordained to be with Him that He could send them, and ordained to be fruitful. What a life! And Jesus Christ is the same, yesterday, today and forever. We are not left out: we are in it. He calleth His own sheep by name and they follow Him, and no one is mistaken when they see them. Jesus said: "By their fruit ye shall know them." There is no mistake about it, we are known by our fruit.

Two young men and a young woman stood in front of the bungalow: they had traveled over 800 miles to get here. I went out to greet them. They looked very confused and unhappy, and the young woman had a defiant expression on her face.

They were two brothers and a sister. They said they were

Christians. They had brought their sister; would we take her in? Then the elder brother produced a letter from a far-away friend telling me their story. It was sordid enough and gave much food for thought.

Here was a girl born and brought up in a Christian family: her parents were Christians: her father died when she was about six years old: she went to a Mission School and read from class to class until she was 16 years of age. She meant to go further, but her summer holiday that year changed all her plans, for she spent those weeks with their sister who was married to a Hindu, and he had taken a great fancy to her: he was rich, he could give her anything she desired, there was good living in a big house, and a life of poverty was changed for a life of ease and luxury, and it didn't take long to persuade her to see the advantage of becoming a Hindu. She had known nothing but poverty all her life. The Mission friends had paid for her education. She had been brought up in their school, had passed her examinations year by year, was trained in the Christian doctrine and had read her Bible every day. She had learned a great deal about the Lord Jesus Christ, went to church every Sunday when she was in school, and was to all appearances a Christian, but she had never been convicted of sin, never felt her need of a Saviour, never been born again. She was a living illustration of those words: "That which is born of the flesh is flesh," and we felt our own need in the face of it. Yes, we could and would take her in if she were willing to come in—and she showed her willingness by stepping forward!

I think she was tired and she wanted to get away from her brothers who spoke as if they had a right over her. Anyhow, she came in, and I put her to live with Lotus, while her brothers had rooms outside the compound. She said that she was *not* a Christian, she was a Hindu—so that would break her caste, and so I asked her how she became Hindu. She said that the man she had lived with made her one! She was not going to eat food with us, so I said very quietly to her, "No one will make you eat food here if you do not wish to. You are perfectly free—we only want to help you." And then she gave me her Hindu name, and I wrote it down, but I also asked for her Christian name, which she refused to give, so I left her to think it over.

Lotus came to talk things over with me the next day. She was very concerned because the girl refused to eat, and she said she would not stay here. So I told the girl's story to her, adding: "She needs to be convicted of sin, and only the Holy Spirit can do that: we must get down before the Lord and make sure that we are filled with His Spirit, and then He can do His work. 'When He is come He will convict,' and I think the responsibility is here: it rests with us, we must give ourselves to prayer." I can see the understanding in the face of our Lotus as I think back: she knew, she understood, and she set to work to make a highway for our God. Nothing daunted her—no ill manner, or rudeness or refusal to share our life took the edge from her keenness: she came back and back again to me to pray, and she firmly believed and watched for the answer.

But there was no sign of repentance and no intimation that food would be acceptable, and at the end of the second day there was distress in the Nurseries because the new sister still refused to eat.

"What shall we do?" they said to me, and I answered: "Why should she eat if she doesn't want to? Leave her alone to fast if she wants to. There is much in the Bible about fasting, so it must be a very good thing," and I tried to appear casual, but my heart was asking God to deal with the situation, and I was watching to see how He would do it. Lotus was very distressed when three days passed and she still held out, and so I sat down with her and we faced the situation again together.

"I believe it all depends upon us," I said to her, "and if the Holy Spirit can have all there is of us He will work. He must see that there is no impatience, no lack of love, no hardness, no complaining, or we shall grieve Him, and how can He speak to her through us if we are thinking of ourselves?" And together we waited before the Lord, and He stilled us and filled our hearts with love for her.

Over and over again the girl came to my room to say that she would not stay with us: her brothers saw her every day, and the old defiance remained. "We will see what we can do and when we have found a safe place for you, your brothers will take you," I assured her, and that satisfied her for the moment. *And*—another day passed, but almost at eleven o'clock the next day I saw her walking across the compound towards my room.

She walked straight to me, looked at me, then bowed her head and stood—she was silent and I waited for her to speak—and suddenly I felt the presence of the Lord. I knew His Spirit had come to set her free if she were willing to let Him. So I talked to her of the past and reminded her of all the teaching she had had through the years in school. I spoke to her of the missionary who had known her from her childhood. "I have visited that school," I said. "I know that you know the way of life, and that there is no need for me to tell you about it. I know that you know about prayer in the Name of Jesus. I know that you can read your Bible, and that you know right from wrong. What has led you to the state you are in now?" And very softly I called her by her Christian name and reminded her of the prayers that had been prayed for her all through the years, and then I asked the question: "When are you going to pray?" She stood in silence by my table and I waited for the answer. I noticed a movement of her head, and her hands clasped and unclasped, and again I repeated the name she had received at her baptism and great tear-drops fell on the floor.

"Shall I pray?" I asked, and promptly she knelt by my side and her pent-up feelings were poured out like a torrential flood! She had sinned, she knew it; she had followed her own way and it had led her into the depths that she could not get out of. "Oh, if only Thou wilt save me," she cried, "if only Thou wilt help me," she wailed, "I do want to be a Christian and I am lost—"

I waited with her while she poured her heart out before the Lord. She made no excuses for herself, she was convicted of sin. It was all exactly as Jesus said: "When He (The Holy Spirit) is come, He will convict of sin." The Holy Spirit was at work, and for two hours she was held to her decision, and I knelt with her praying, waiting, and watching to see what He would do while He brought to her remembrance the things that led her astray.

It is with solemn awe I tell you this story: her long, uninterrupted confession of self-seeking to satisfy herself at all costs had reached a climax: she was arrested by the Holy Spirit. Lotus had opened her heart wide to Him, He had come in, and He was working through her, searching, convicting, and convincing. The girl prayed it all out, and then heaving a deep sigh, she lay down where she was, and fell asleep. There was a rug near: I threw it over her, and she slept for hours.

Early that evening I called Lotus and asked her to prepare some food, for I felt sure she would need it when she awoke.

"It is all ready," she replied. "I saw your door shut and I knew in my spirit that Jesus had triumphed, so I prepared nice tasty food that she will like: it is all ready for her when she awakes." She looked at me with radiant understanding, for glory filled her soul. We had seen the Word of God fulfilled and a miracle performed.

The girl awoke to a new life: all the defiance was gone: arrogance and pride were exchanged for humility, and I walked with her into the Nurseries, saw the welcoming smiles she received, and a hand stretched out in silent love and understanding to lead her to the place where food was ready to be put before her, and there I left them.

I went into my room to read again that simple record of Jesus preparing a meal for His weary disciples, and I sat back to think about it and to try to visualize it. In holy awe I pictured Him lighting the fire, cleaning and cooking the fish, making bread for them, and when their hunger was satisfied, sitting down with them and asking the question that has gripped us through the years, "Peter, do you love Me more than these?" What is the answer? Listen: "Lord, thou knowest that I love Thee." But it didn't stop at that: there must be a practical expression, and Peter heard Jesus say to him, "Then feed my lambs, and feed my sheep." The dawn of that day brought a real understanding to Peter of what love is and must do. Real love is practical, and often is shown in the way we prepare a meal, but love unexpressed will die, and no one will be warmed by it.

Then I thought of Lotus and how really she had manifested His Spirit. The sin-sick weary child of His was revived--a new life filled her being, and she stepped out to follow Him. Lotus had prayed to be filled with the Holy Spirit--God had given to her that which she asked of Him, and I sat before Him, satisfied. I had seen the glory of the Lord in the land of the living, but that was not the end, for the girl arose and began to minister, and very soon she asked to be trained to serve.

I wrote to a friend who understands, and she was accepted in the Bible School.

That happened years ago. She is now the mother of a family, and the wife of a pastor, and because she has been saved from much, she has loved much through the years.

Her elder brother went back to his work, while the younger one was drifting about with nothing particular to do. He did odd jobs, but was not trained to earn his living. Though he was too poor to pay for the training, a few questions revealed the fact that his desire was to do carpentry.

I sat down with him and talked of Jesus in His home in Nazareth, and we tried to picture the things He made in the carpenter's shop, and almost before I knew it, the lad was saying: "Oh, I would like to be like Him: oh, it would be wonderful if I could learn to do as He did!" And it seemed the most natural thing in the world for him to kneel down there and ask the Saviour of men to create in him a clean heart and to put a right spirit within him and make him a good man. There is a place we know that has become famous for the excellent furniture they turn out, so I wrote there and he was accepted at once. It is wonderful how the way opened and how the money came to pay his expenses, but what else could we expect when his desire was only to make things as Jesus did? And now——? he is a master workman, and a member of the Church Council where he lives. His new life opened up a way of great opportunities, and sometimes he goes out with the Evangelistic Band to tell others what Jesus is waiting to do for them.

🜲 3 🜲

PRAYER

"THE EFFECTUAL FERVENT *prayer of a righteous man availeth much." --James 5:16.*

Teach me to pray--What shall I pray?
Lord teach me what it means,
To pray the effectual fervent prayer,
That "IS" just what it seems.
A truthful prayer a fervent prayer,
A prayer with all of me,
Just one big longing in the cry,
My Father, God to Thee.
Dear God, I want to pray the prayer--
Cost what it will to me—
That must avail, that will prevail,
When I cry out to Thee.
For oh! The need on every hand!
Lives broken down by sin;
Wandering they go, far from the Fold,
Lord teach me pray them in.
Make me a righteous man who prays,
For others in distress,

Thy will, oh Lord, for them be done,
Thy will, and nothing less.
The fervent prayer availing much;
Effectual prayer be mine,
Lord pray in me all Thy desire,
The prayer, Lord, that is Thine
O teach me, Lord, to pray right through,
And Victory I can see,
Where praise is heard and prayer is lost
In praise and love to Thee.

❧ 4 ❧

I AM REDEEMED

I T WAS SUNDAY MORNING, the sun rose in fiery heat, and there was nothing refreshing to begin the day. We hear much about the cool of dawn, but we felt nothing of it that day. I was hot and sticky and tired, and yet the day lay before us. I was staying in Peace Cottage: nothing could be more like its name, but that did not cool the atmosphere. I looked across the garden to the ploughed-up compound where we were preparing for a harvest of wheat, and my eyes wandered over the land where rice was growing and on to the lentil bushes, and I began to think of the vital truth Jesus declared: "Whatsoever a man soweth, *that* shall he also reap."

This we naturally expect in the garden, in the compound, and in the fields: but we sometimes forget that other sowing--of deeds and words--and we neither look for nor expect a harvest. Yet that doesn't alter the fact, and I am perfectly sure that we reap what we sow—*that* and nothing else. No time or distance or circumstance ever alters the fact. Every day we sow thoughts and words and actions, and we cannot escape the harvest. It is as sure as the dawn.

I thought much about it when I first came to India 36 years

ago, and I followed in the train of those who had made a way for me. "We are sowers," said the Biblewomen, "the people listen well." And I heard this so often that I began to wonder whether anybody thought of a harvest. We walked through the fields divided by little mud tracks and we remarked about the growing grain. A man was ploughing one field, another was riding a flat piece of wood over the ploughed-up land, leveling and preparing for the seed to be sown, and then we arrived at a tiny village sheltered in trees, and the first house we visited belonged to the farmer who owned the fields. The folk there were busy, looking over the seed to be sown, and I sat down and watched them there. They talked as they worked, but their eyes were on the seed. "It is good seed," said the wife of the farmer. "It is the best," said the farmer, and the family group held out their hands full of g rain to show me, and those with me, that they knew what they were talking about.

Then they paused as I looked, and turning to the farmer I asked: "What do you expect? What are you preparing for?" He looked at me with a strange look, and then came nearer. His hand rested on a pile on the floor: he put his fingers in the grain and let it filter through as he spoke. "This is the best wheat in these parts. I shall sow this in *that* field," he said, pointing to where the bullocks were ploughing and the ground was being prepared, "and I shall have the best wheat field for miles round."

"How do you know?" I asked, and he screwed his lips and looked out through the village, and I think he concluded that a very silly woman was visiting his house that day. But after a time, he said under his breath as he played with the prepared grain on the floor. "When I want good wheat, I sow good wheat: when I want a cheap kind, I sow a cheap kind. I know what I shall get, and I know which I like best."

I began to talk with the women. They were all very interested in what they were doing, and they joyed in assurance of a harvest even before they had sown the seed. I watched them for a long time. Questions and answers were passed between the two Biblewomen with me and that busy household, and then there was a pause, and I said that I had a Book with me that contained wonderful words from God. He had spoken, Holy men had heard Him and written down His words, and there was something about a harvest. "There is always a harvest," I remarked. "It is sure, and we are preparing for it. 'What shall it profit a man if he gain the whole world and lose his own soul, or what will a man give in exchange for his soul?'" I opened the Book and looked—yes, those were the words written there, and I paused. Then I turned over the leaves and read the record of the man who knew how to grow good things, and who was such a successful farmer that his idea of getting rich possessed him and he said: "I will build greater barns." He knew he could fill them, but, while he worked and planned and schemed for the increase of his worldly store, in the silence of the evening he heard a voice. He had not given a thought to the possibility of never seeing the harvest. Supposing God called him—what then? How would he respond? And there in that garner we talked of life and of death and after that the judgment.

They had never heard the story of Jesus and knew nothing about God's plan of salvation, but they listened, and they asked questions. The farmer understood, for he said under his breath: "When I want good wheat I sow good grain and I get the good harvest." Yes, it is true: "Whatsoever a man soweth, *that* shall he also reap," and I went out to watch the men and women working in the fields. There was plenty to do before the seed was sown-- much toil, and long hot days hard at it, and *then,* the sowing. We talked of this as we walked through the fields, and when we got to the next village we prayed with the people. We came out to teach, but *we* were being taught. God was speaking to our hearts, showing us that if we wanted a harvest, we much prepare for it, and at the close of the day I went home to think—what we had seen that day had stirred our imagination. We talk so glibly of being sent to preach and we begin to learn the language with that end in view, and the difficulties of the way are increasing as the days go by and are not over even when we can speak with new tongues.

There is so much left out of the curriculum in the missionary training, so much left unsaid, and yet so absolutely necessary to every one who is entrusted with the word of reconciliation—and—yet—and—yet, it is written in the Book. "If only someone had told us," we say, "if only we had been taught to wait on the Lord, if only someone had said: 'You must learn to tarry.'" We are so eager to be on the move, there is no stillness about us, and although we bring the glad tidings of peace, we don't know very much about it. We talk of what we have learned and know, and the people pause to listen, but they are not gripped. We tell them the story of Redeeming Love, but there is no power in what we say. It is all true, it is all good, and we were serious about our calling and the message we were sent to give, and yet—we had forgotten or we were ignorant of that vital preparation, the enduement with power from on high. As we walked the ways of failure wondering why, trying to learn, struggling to know, reading books that explain the way of life: reading, praying and working, and achieving nothing that is worth recording, we grew weary trying. Why? Because we thought that we would get there, and we didn't—power is *not* learned--power is given--it has to be received and it comes with enduement from on high.

Power comes to those who wait upon the Lord. It is given to those who tarry in His presence, to those who have asked and who wait until they receive, and the place where we knelt to pray becomes the Holy of Holies, and we say, in the words of the Psalmist, "I waited for the Lord, He heard my prayer," and we wait to listen to Him "I heard the voice of Jesus say, 'I am this dark world's Light'"--our perspective is changed, and we wonder how His light can penetrate such dense darkness: but as we pray and wait before Him, there is revealed to us the blessed truth that it is only through and by the coming of the Holy Ghost, revealing Jesus, the Light of the World, bringing Life and immortality to the people to whom we are set, *then* the words that He gives--they are spirit and they are life--and we can go out with joy and be led forth with singing to see for ourselves that instead of briars and thorns and wilderness growth there is a harvest field.

I was thinking over these things, for they are tested and tried. He taught me when I prayed to Him, and answered beyond my wildest dreamings. OH! How I longed to see souls born again: I toiled and sought and wept and prayed, and then one day He came to me and said: "Ask of Me and I will give thee the heathen for thine inheritance and the uttermost parts of the earth for thy possession," and there I knelt in His presence until my being was filled with awe and I stayed to worship, and from that day I realized that prayer must be the fundamental part of my life: it could no longer be supplemental to what I did, and I began to rise before the dawn just to meet Him: and He is not a disappointment--prayer changed things, prayer changed me, and the harvest has been just as He said according to His Word all through these years. I sat thinking on these things, marveling at the goodness of God, and suddenly I remembered that across the compound in a room prepared, there was to be a gathering together of those who know and love Him--a Feast of Remembrance, Holy Communion some people call it--but we call it "The Breaking of the Bread service," and there is a solemn awe in the walk of those who are going.

I left Peace Cottage and walked to "Zion," and into that holy stillness I stepped to a seat where no one had to pass me, and gave myself up to meditation. After a while, I opened my eyes and looked over the rows of girls just entering womanhood. Their heads were bowed. They sat on the floor in true Eastern fashion. At the back sat a converted Sadhu and his wife: to the right of them sat our Lotus: and round the wall were those of us who find it difficult to squat right on the ground. "Who are these arrayed in white and whence came they?" you will ask. And I answer: "They have everyone suffered: they have every one been washed in the Blood of the Lamb. They came there because they have heard the voice of Jesus: they opened their hearts to Him and He has come in. He has won their heart's affections, and they are there as an expression of their love. They are saved to serve, the children the Good Shepherd brought to us. They have been through the class-rooms and some of them through training school: they are grown up now and in love they serve." All heads are bowed, all eyes closed, and there is a silence that is felt.

As I said before, I was sitting where no one could pass me and I gave myself up to medication: and then, just as if something had broken the windows of heaven to let the glory out, a sweet voice began to sing: "Nor silver nor gold hath obtained my redemption." Before the end of the line all there had joined in song: the harmony, in the part singing, was heavenly music. I tried to sing, but I couldn't a lump filled my throat, tears rolled down my face, and I wept as they sang, "It was the precious Blood of Jesus that took my sin away." "Nor silver nor gold hath obtained my redemp-tion," the voices repeated, and I wept tears of unspeakable joy. Jesus Himself drew near, and as we partook of the Bread, He made Himself known to us. The service is pure worship. The one who ministered to us was once a caste Hindu--now a bondslave of Jesus Christ—and somehow or other as the wine was poured into the cup we seemed to hear a voice saying "Take—drink—this is My Blood which was shed for you"—and again they sang.

I am redeemed, but not with silver,
I am bought, but not with gold;
Bought with a price, the Blood of Jesus,
Precious price of love untold.

And I partook of the Bread and the Wine with a vivid revela-tion of what it cost for us all to be there.

The service was over and I walked across the garden to be alone and think: but I heard Flower singing in the compound as I passed by the wall:

Not silver nor gold hath obtained my redemption,
No riches of earth could have saved my poor soul,
The Blood of the Cross is my only foundation,
The death of my Saviour now maketh me whole,
I am redeemed—

and my thoughts were of her. One day, a long time ago, she was a child widow. At the time of her husband's death she went with her mother to the place where his body was to burn. She was meant to bury with him, but a miracle happened and the mother and child escaped, and in a very round-about way they came to us. But the mother had suffered more than she could bear and she lay down to wait for the end, while we told her of Jesus, the Mighty to save. She was found of Him, the eyes of her heart were opened and she saw Him--her Redeemer--for her heaven opened and, one day, she went in. But her child is still with us, now a dignified Christian young woman, working with us, testifying by her life and lip that Jesus saves and keeps: and her fingers express her love in the garments she makes for the family. It is a wonderful thing to be redeemed: it is a marvelous thing to be kept by the power of God.

Every one in that Breaking of Bread service has been redeemed. I knew every one of them, they are the children God has given to me, and the evening of my life is made rich by them. When God called me to be a missionary, I never dreamed of such love. I had no idea of the wonders before me or of the glory I should see, but every promise He made to me has been fulfilled. He has increased my joy in the Lord, and given to me the unspeakable bliss of belonging entirely to Him. The passing years have increased His preciousness to me and I know that it is better on before, because He is there. Could anything be better? I look back and say to you: 'It is wonderful to be a missionary: it is a life without regrets. But—

Wherever you ripe fields behold,
Waving to God their sheaves of gold,
Be sure, some corn or wheat has died,
Some soul has there been crucified.
Someone has wrestled, wept, and prayed,
And fought hell's legions undismayed,
There is no gain without a loss,
You cannot save but by a cross.
And the finest wheat held in your hand will bring no harvest:

you must give it up to be sown. If it dies--much fruit. The ground must be cleared and cleaned, before it is ploughed, and much time given to preparation, and when all is ready, "Whatsoever a man soweth, *that* shall he also reap."

God's Word to Me
"Whatsoever ye shall ask the Father in My
Name THAT will I do."-John 14:13.
If ye shall ask anything in My Name,
I will do it."- 14:14
This is not random speaking,
This is God's Word to me,
That whatsoever I shall ask,
In Jesus' Name, His Blessed Name,
He will give that to me.
With love and understanding,
Of all I need just now
For anything, whate'er I ask,
In Jesus 'Name, His Precious Name,
By faith He gives me now.
I stand upon His promise,
I know no other way,
No other plea, no other name,
But Jesus' Name, In Jesus' Name,
God answers when I pray.

HE GAVE AS HE SAID

T IS RAINING and a cool breeze is blowing, which is a great cheer: but yesterday brought great joy to us. It was only an airgraph and the joy in the heart of the writer filled our hearts too. We could almost hear the shout of victory, and distance vanished in the joy with you all over the conquered foe--flying bombs, the so-called doodles--are mastered! The sleepless nights on account of them are over--there is peace in the heart before peace is declared. We have followed you in all your tribulation as far as we could, and we have watched to see what God would do. The writer of yesterday's airgraph has lived in London all through the war: she wrote once that she had just jumped up to see where a bomb had fallen. There was a roar, a silence, and then a great cloud of dust rising--she had seen it all--it was so near: and she has been kept in peace all through because God had said to her, "With Me shalt thou be in safeguard," and she has tested it out. Isn't it wonderful that He can, and does, so garrison a heart? Is it any wonder that we long that others be led to know Him too? And we make it our business in life to talk about Jesus! The arrow has flown by day--the destruction has been there by night--and they are not overwhelmed. The terrible reality of war has been ever present, and yet--they write of miracles, they tell us of deliverances, and they send help to us.

There was one terrible night when the house rocked and buildings around them fell, and it was a night to be remembered: yet, early next morning, this friend went to the bank and cabled out money to help the needy in India. Someone said, "I'd like to send some money for the children," and another said, "I will give." In their sorrow and calamity they thought of others 7,000 miles away, and the givers are a mixed crowd. Their names are written in God's Book of Remembrance. The news passed round, and an invalid who cannot run to a shelter (she has heart trouble) but can write cheques, wrote one there. A missionary on furlough gave three English pounds. An old lady aged 91, opened her box in triumph and produced some coins. "I have earned it all myself," she said. She is blind, but she can knit dishcloths.

Another friend lives in a far-away village where she has a tiny shop displayed in her cottage window--her goods for sale are odds and ends of stamps for collectors, and she sent five English pounds. Think of the care and the love involved! Two elderly ladies sent 30 shillings, and one who must earn money to get her daily food gave sixpence out of her daily pay. Three others gave eight shillings, and one who is passing through the valley of Baca has made it a well, and she sent 10 shillings, and one I do not know gave: and early in May from that house in London, surrounded by devastation they see every day, they sent 20 pounds, and we received it in the days of trial for us. We were facing the fact of shortage and God was saying to us: "The trial of your faith being much more precious than gold." That money arrived to remind us that we are being tried. It also said: "Your heavenly Father knoweth." We looked into our ways and asked ourselves vital questions, and then we read again of the feeding of five thousand people with five loaves and two small fishes. Anyhow, the 20 English pounds was two small fishes--where was the other to come from? We looked into the story again, and we saw the record--a small boy here and he had five loaves and two fishes--that's all.

It is such a laughable thing to talk about in the face of all those people, and a good many people would say, "What is the good of that? Talk with some sense: you must be practical." And everybody begins to say, "What shall we do?" And Jesus sees it all. "How many have you?" He asks. "Go and see," and He took command of the situation. Well, we were exactly like that--and when we had counted all we had and added the 20 English pounds just arrived, there was enough and to spare: but it needed all those odd little sums and the price of the dishcloths knitted by a blind lady, to say nothing of the lady who bravely keeps shop: and all we had, to feed the family here and to pay the fees for those away that month, and when all was given to Jesus He took it into His hands and blessed it, and we saw for ourselves that Jesus Christ is the same, yesterday and today. He has not changed, and "His grace and power are such, None can ever ask too much." "Those who trust Him wholly, find Him wholly true."

Bua sings her song of joy, "The Lord is *my* Shepherd, there's nothing short"--and then goes into reminiscence. "I remember," she says, "when there was nothing, and we had to live in a hired dwelling, and God gave all this," waving her hands round. "He told us that if we brought all our tithes into the storehouse and proved Him, He would open the windows of heaven and pour out so much, there would not be room to contain it, and so we began to pay our tithes. Some of us were afraid that we would not have enough when we had done that." Then, in a confidential tone, nodding as she spoke. "One rupee out of ten is rather much" she said, and I agreed with her: yet God had said a tenth, so we would give it and prove Him. Her face lit up. "Hai, hai," she said, "it has all been so wonderful: first He gave houses, then He filled them, and we kept singing, 'I'm treading on the upward way, new lessons learning every day.' Yes, I remember when there was nothing, and *now*--see--there is the bungalow. God told that kind Sahib and Memsahib in England to send the money so that you could build it."

I thought of the day when the letter came from Captain and

Mrs. Dawson telling me how, as they prayed, God spoke to them both and the 1,000 English pounds was put on one side for me. It was to build a bungalow and quarters for six Biblewomen and Teachers. I was ill with joy--it was too high for me. We had prayer and God had answered--how? Exactly as he promised--according to His riches in glory. We needed a place to live in with arrangements for our Indian fellow-workers. I asked the Resident Engineer how much money we required to do the whole thing, and he calculated that 800 English pounds would do it. It is enough to make anybody laugh that we should even think of such a thing, but so much depended on the life and work here, and I had no idea then what God was leading me to. We gave ourselves to prayer, and I always find that prayer leads to the path of obedience--there is no evading it--it was a definite challenge then, and as I prayed, two of us (both missionaries), one in Benares and one here, gave what we had to start off, and it was only 7 English punds in all, and what is that to pay for buildings costing 800 English pounds? It was ridiculous—and—yet there was God and He watched to see what we would do. 800 English pounds and we had seven English pounds! How can we get the money? Thoughts ran riot. It would take a long time to collect it, and how could I ask people for it? If I told some rich people about it and asked them to pray for it, wouldn't it be a round-about way of asking them to give it? No, that didn't seem right. I knew that God could supply it all and I felt sure He would, but what did He want me to do about it? I could seek guidance and wait for it, and I did--and it came in quite an unexpected way.

Five of us were talking about needs and telling of various ways and means, and of course the subject of the bungalow and quarters for our Indian fellow-workers was discussed. We went out and walked round the compound, looked at the dilapidated buildings, and I ventured: "We want better buildings to house suitable teachers for the work crying out to be done. The need is imperative." We stood there under the lovely blue sky and pondered. "The roof of the bungalow descends in the monsoon and we have cans scattered on the floor to catch the water—it's a miserable affair when it gets to the bedrooms, and though it may raise laughter to tell that we go to bed with an umbrella to shelter us from the rain in the night, the fun of it evaporates after a time, and I'd like a roof that stays up, instead of the one made of tiles stuck together with mud that melts in the deluge." We had a good laugh together as we told of our experiences and then we went in to supper. It was after that, that the guidance came.

"How much will it cost to put up new buildings?" one of the party asked, and I answered what the Chief Engineer had esti-mated—800 English pounds. "How much have you towards it?" he questioned, and I answered, "seven." There was a great laugh: we all laughed together, and I felt the laugh was against me—it was absurd I knew—and yet a laugh never hurt anybody. "How are you going to get the rest?" was the next question. It takes a long time to raise money nowadays—and then fear gripped me. Fear that I should not reach the place I wanted in the life of Faith—and I said as bravely as I could, "If the Lord Jesus could feed five thousand men and with five loaves and two fishes He could make seven pounds enough for what we need. I'll ask Him to do it. There was silence for a while. Everybody was thinking. "I'm afraid you will be a long time getting it," said one of the party, and I—stirred to action by the laugh against me—replied: "I never thought of getting it all myself. I will ask God to tell one person to give it all": and then we sat down and opened our Bibles while the man of the company read to us the words of Life. Then we knelt to pray, and it was as we prayed that guidance came. Faith was something bigger than anything we had thought of or talked about, and I heard a voice saying to me: "My God shall supply all your need according to His riches in glory by Christ Jesus." It came with such power and conviction that all my being rose in thankfulness to God. I knew He would give: I was sure He would give more than the 800 pounds needed, because the promised supply was to be according to His riches in glory: and that was more than just enough.

When we had prayed we rose to face each other and I thanked them for laughing at me. One of them said how sorry they were they had done so, but I answered: "Oh, don't be sorry, it has done me good. It drove me to be definite and believe to see, and I believe the miracle will be performed. How? I do not know. Jesus does, and I am sure He will do what we have asked." And that was the end of the asking for *that*. Exactly eight months after that night the answer came, and as I said before, I was ill with the joy of it. The two letters I received then are before me now. The first, "Why did you not tell me of your need?" The second, "I am glad you did not tell us of your need, I like to feel sure that God spoke to us both at the same time and told us exactly how much to send." And that was the way Captain and Mrs. Dawson gave to us the very beginnings of what is now called "The Nurseries," Gorakhpu. The answer to our prayer was 1,000 pounds—200 more than we asked for!

Bua speaks of the way God our Father leads: she has been with me from the beginning. There is nothing hazy about her state-ments--facts are facts, and she gives all the glory to God: and we are "still treading the upward way, new lessons learning every day." Then and now have only proved to me and those with me here that God is able to fulfill every promise He has made, and there is no want to them that trust Him. I think of the army of His lovers in England who know his voice and who hearken and heed, and I look round the compound and watch little children play, and young women busy in their love service, and then I look up and say, "Father, I thank Thee."

Captain and Mrs. Dawson have joined the Church Triumphant, their bliss is complete, they are with Christ which is far better. They left to me a sacred trust in these buildings to live in. But I know *that* money was first given to God, and I sometimes wonder how much they know of how He has used and blessed and hallowed their gift. There is the feeling always that this is God's house, and I heard Bertha telling the children the other day that we must all make the compound clean and beautiful for Him, and the children moved in abandonment to the joy of it. Sacred gifts are sacred, and they bring the Shekinah glory over the place. It is here, just here, that I have seen the glory of the Lord in the land of the living. Hundreds have been born again, and a good many have heard the voice of God and obeyed to go out to seek and to save that which was lost from this place they gave. The little gifts and the big gifts feed the hungry and clothe the naked: love given finds love's answer in other lives, and Jesus calls these givers the blessed of His Father. Read the story again and find out for yourself whether you are described in that discourse.

T*he Greatest is Love*
Love of my love, come nearer,
Nearer, nearer still,
Let us give love's own giving,
Love's meaning to fulfill.
Love of my life, speechless I stand,
But Thou dost know and understand.
Oh, Love of loves, I cry to Thee,
In love's own cry of ecstasy,
Love of my life, I Thee adore,
Oh give me power to love thee more.

❧ 6 ❧

AND NOW

S HE IS JUST BACK--SHE arrived last evening--her Miss Sahib has given her a month's holiday--so she has come home. I looked at her radiant face and listened to her confident words. She has been away for a year and has tested the promises of God. And now--she knows--and it is not just what we say--it is "thus saith the Lord," and her heart is in her words. "What about Lalita?" I ask, and her question is, "What do you think?' "Her training is only half way through. We must pray and ask the Lord what His will is for her." "Yes, that is it," she answered. "He knows what He wants, we can ask and wait." And then she talked of her other children, all doing well, and giving joy to their widowed mother. "You will be able to go out and give your testimony while you are here, won't you?"--and putting my hand on her shoulder, I looked into her face and said: "God can do a great deal in a month." We stood for a minute in silence, then I mentioned a name very dear to her. "She comes sometimes," I said. "Perhaps she is waiting for you to show her the way. She has been-- she knows--and God has sent you here--we will pray." "Yes, we will pray. I know what the Lord Jesus is to me and I can tell her that"-- and we moved out into the compound. "What He is to me, I can tell her *that*," I repeated to myself, and I wondered how many people who read these words would go out and tell others just what He is to them. Testimonies are needed--someone to give their witness. It is marvelous in its results, for God says, "a true witness delivereth souls!"

The name of the woman I have just mentioned means "something fair," and that is not the colour of her skin but she knows what it is to pray, and has seen the answer. When she first came here with her little family--she wasn't sure of staying--she came for safety, for her husband had died suddenly--and bereft of the supplier of the family needs, what could she do? She knew of a woman who had changed her religion and become a Christian and could earn her living now. She made inquiries and walked the long weary miles over the fields until she arrived outside our compound.

She sat on a bit of wall by the roadside with her children close around her. They were a sad-looking crowd and one of them was very sick, and while she waiting a familiar voice spoke to her, asked her what she was doing, where she was going, and the woman she was seeking was there in the way talking to her. "Come in with me," she said, "come and rest, and we can talk and I will prepare food." Kind words opened the floodgates, and tears rained down her face, as she entered the door of the courtyard. "I am a widow," she wailed, "bereft, with four children," and they drew closer to her, while her story was told to a heart "at leisure from itself." They were not strangers, they knew each other in that far-away village in the days of long ago, but a change had come to them both--one had left home and kindred seeking the way of salvation. She had found it and was ready to help this friend of bygone days. There was no stint in her giving, for when India gives, she gives without measure, lavishly, unsparingly, and not always counting the cost. The feast was prepared for that widow and her four children. I wonder what she thought of the change in the woman who was once a caste Hindu in her village, now preparing food for her. "You can stay the night, and then tomorrow we shall see what you want to do. We can pray and God will answer and He will show you. After food you must rest." And she busied herself preparing a place that might be a haven of peace for a short while. They feasted and they rested and the woman who had taken them in and fed them, shut her door to think.

"I have not told Mamaji, I have not told anybody, now--what shall I do?" she questioned herself. "It is not safe for a widow to wander in the city. I can keep her tonight, five of them, but tomorrow, they will know what to do. God will show them"--a widow with four children is very much! And as she thought, she prayed. She was very simple. She could neither read nor write. She had tried to learn both, but her brain did not work that way. She could do other things, and her deeds could be trained into a channel of blessing, and so, she became an Aunt in the family.

Everything was done so quietly, so unobtrusively, that no one knew until the following day what had happened. The Aunt was entering her compound door and on her way to the Nurseries where she hoped to find me. "I have some visitors," she announced. "They are from my village. They have come to see, and are waiting to see you"--and the family paused to hear the announcement. "I knew you had visitors," said old Bua, "bring them in": and to the surprise of all, the Aunt went to her house and the widow and her children were brought in. She looked bewildered, but our children came forward in friendly fashion to have a good look at the arrivals, and I think they knew more than they said. The amazing questions these people ask unabashed--nothing seems too private or too intimate to ask about, and the marvel to me is that they are answered just as they are asked, and no one seems to mind. Private lives are made public. Some people say that there are no secrets in India, but I think they know better. Life for a widow with four children cannot be very secret: she has to face the fact of life and how to live, and our visitor was taking her surroundings and looking at our children when a bell rang, and the family moved on. She saw them assemble in long lines near the Bungalow, and watched them walking to the place of worship. "We begin the day with prayer," said Bua, and the widow turned round to see the last child enter the Praise Hall.

Bua sat with her and I left them to talk, while I went to morning worship with the Teachers. Life is very full and exacting and yet, could anything be more satisfying? We prayed for our new visitors, asking God to meet them here, and then they all went off to the city--some to schools, some to Zenanas, and their day's work began.

The compound was on the move too, and even tiny people have duties to perform which they think are very important--and they are--a number of little folk have each got a rose tree or a flowering shrub to water every morning. They carry little buckets to the pump which some bigger girl fills with water, and what is not spilled on the way may be poured on the shrub or rose tree: some get nearly drowned, others are fairly watered, and some just miss the mark. So our roses and flowering shrubs are not all equal, but the little people who busy themselves are very important, and they begin the day after prayers, with a good half hour in the garden. It is good health-giving service and brings its own reward. The widow sat with Bua talking over things as they are. "I must do something," she said. "I must work: how can I feed my children?" she asked, and they sat pondering ways and means, when the Aunt came to call her for her meal. "What a number of children there are here" she remarked. "They all wear clothes, and even little children know how to water the garden. Oh, I wish I could stay here: I could work, and my children could help. Oh, I wish I could stay here, but what can I do?" That evening her remarks were repeated to me, and we prayed to know how best to help her and we asked ourselves, "What would Jesus do?" If we took her in, it would be five more people to feed and to clothe: but if God had sent them, what then? Was He not responsible? And we asked ourselves again, "What would Jesus do?" The widow decided for herself, and next morning, she asked me for work to do, and I sat down to talk with her. She listened with wondering eyes as I told her about Jesus and read those wonderful words:

"Come unto me all ye that are weary and heavy laden and I will give you rest."

I said to her: "I believe God has sent you here. He gave His only begotten Son to save you: it is He Who said those words I read from the Book. He cares for you, and I will ask Him to make Himself known to you while you are here." Her eyes opened wide in astonishment, but she said nothing. So we knelt and prayed, and she went off to talk things over with the Aunt and the children.

A week passed and she was working in the compound. Another week and her children were in the class rooms. They had settled in! They were watching to see how the supply of their need would come, and one day as she walked across the compound, I met her, and she asked me. I took her aside and explained to her that our God is the God of the widow and the Father of the fatherless. "And He cares for you," I said again. We talked of the fields around the village she had left, we talked of the birds that flew over it, and we read words from the Book that brought conviction, and she began to see.

Weeks and months passed by and she was still with us. Her attitude to life was very changed: she no longer wailed out her sorrow: she looked upon her children with adoring eyes: she was a real illustration of the word, "having food and raiment we are content." She was, but I was not: how could I be? She was changed, very changed, but she was not born again, and I knew that that was her great need; how was she to feel it? I sat and thought about it. I prayed for her, and then I explained that living with us did not make her a Christian "I am a Hindu," she said. "All my children are born Hindus. How can we be anything else?" she asked; and there, just there, the Holy Spirit brought to my remembrance words of vital meaning, but we sat together for a long time, and I told her how Jesus said to a man that was not born a Christian: "You must be born again." The man did not understand, and he asked how that could happen to a grown-up man, and Jesus explained by talking about the wind. We talk a great deal about the wind, but no one ever saw it: we look out and we see the trees swaying: we see the flowering shrubs swinging their blossoms: and the dust that was flat on the road suddenly moves rapidly along. "The wind is blowing very fiercely today," someone says. "How do you know?" I ask, and they answer, "*Look*, look out": and I answer, "I cannot see the wind." I know I speak the truth, but I can see work of the wind--drifts of dry leaves, refuse left on the road, carried along by an unseen power, clouds of dust fill the air, a hurricane blows and the wind passes by, and no one has seen it but we all felt it—"It is the wind" we say, and its power was irresistible. "That which is born of the flesh *is* flesh, but that which is born of the spirit *is* spirit." So we need to be born again.

"You are born of the flesh--you need a second birth," I said, and then for some time we sat in silence. I knew she was thinking, I knew she was wondering how these things might be, and I waited there with her, and when the evening shadows began to fall, she slipped away. There was no other talk or questions for some time, but I knew by her manner that she was counting the cost--what would it involve if she took the step? I had told her that if she changed her religion it would mean nothing, but if God changed her, she would have the reality.

She could not remain in ignorance while she lived in the family for they talk of sacred things very naturally. She went to prayers every day. She went into a classroom where others like her learn to read and write and sew. She came in to us, she lived with us, and yet, she was not of us--why? She tried to be, she did all she could to please, never did anyone try harder but—I watched and waited and prayed--watched as one who would have to give an account, waited for the Lord, and prayed for her to be a new creation in Christ Jesus. Then the hot weather came and we melted and wilted while strength evaporated and we had some very sick people in the compound. One of her children was ill when he arrived: we did all we could for him, but the heat was like the blast of the Terrible and it carried away one of her treasures. She looked stunned for a moment—he was her firstborn—and she was dumb in her grief. The family gathered round to comfort and help her, little children slipped their hands into hers and looked into her face with wide open eyes. No one was afraid of death. They think of the Father's House as home, and when someone goes in—well, what could be better? "They will not be sick any more," they say, and there is only gladness that there is such a wonderful place prepared for all who love Him. I believe that sorrow opened her eyes and she saw something of the hope we call blessed, and she began to draw near to God.

Weeks and months passed by and she stayed on--her children were getting on in school, and there was nothing for her to trouble about: but the day of the Lord was at hand. There were meetings for the children taken by the elder girls: there were meetings for the elders taken by one of themselves, and prayer filled the atmosphere, while they gathered together with their Bibles to seek and to find the Lord. One night she sat with her children round her, listening to what was said, when suddenly she said that she felt she was outside. She closed her eyes, she saw a light, and heard a voice unlike any other voice she had ever heard. Someone was reading from the Book. The words she remembered were: "I stand at the door": I knew it was Jesus--"I will come in." "I saw the Light," she said: "I heard the Voice: I felt Him standing there, and I fell on my face and cried out to Him."

He understood her cry, and that night she was born again. We all knew it, we didn't see Him come, but we felt His presence and we saw His work, and for her it was the beginning of a walk in newness of life: old things passed away, all things became new.

She continued with her lessons in the class room: she did her work in the compound, but oh, how different she was, for she walked as seeing Him Who is invisible. She was settled, her heart was at rest, and she applied herself with great zeal to learn to read. She wanted to possess a Bible all her own, and one Christmas I gave her one.

She took it in her hands, held it to her heart, and I opened it for her and she read the wonderful words of life.

We have a training class for women converts, taken by Sister

Thilde, and she went in there, and the messages given were as water to a thirsty soul. We have dispensaries where the sick and need gather for any help we can give, and four miles away there is one where Elise and some of our girls minister, and over eleven thousand from the villages around went there for help last year. It is a marvelous field of blessing, started in a very simple way, and carried on in love's free service.

Sister Thilde taught her class how to give out what they received--the lessons were prepared for simple village women--so they were not too difficult or complicated to grasp. Every one was a definite message, and one day our widow went with another in her class to give to the people who came to the dispensary that which she had learned. Life had a new meaning to her. She soon realized that she was saved to serve, and she went with others to tell the people in the villages what a wonderful Saviour she had found. Her service increased her joy in the Lord and her confidence grew: she was ready for anything ready to go anywhere.

An urgent call for help came from a distant city. We thought of the widow and wondered--she had been with us some years: she was established in the Faith. We told her of the need: she listened and gave herself to prayer. One of her children had passed through the class rooms here and was away in a Training School. Another would soon be going there. There was only her youngest to educate; she was well on: the Lord had done much for her and she was thankful. "If you think that I can do the work and be a help there," she said, "I will go." That was a year ago, and now she is back for a holiday, having proved for herself that when God calls, He enables, and that God's work done in God's way will never lack God's resources.

CLOSE, CLOSE TO THEE

"H E THAT IS JOINED *unto the Lord is
one Spirit.*"--*l Cor. 6:17*
Close, close to Thee,
Oh, precious Lord,
Close, closer still,
According to Thy Word.
Bind all my being,
Close, close to thee,
Joined to Thee only,
Lord, let me be.
"Joined", mystic union,
My soul to Thine.
Thy Blessed Spirit
Conquering mine.
Lost in the Union,
I want to be,
Made one in spirit,
Jesus with Thee.

☙ 8 ❧

CHANGED

S HE HAS JUST BEEN to say "Salaam" to me before she begins her work in the dispensary. I have heard her give her testimony to those village women waiting for the medicine, and it is a vivid story, so told that you can see it.

Her life began in a far-away village of a distant Province. She as like any other Hindu girl born in a Hindu home, prepared from babyhood for the marriage her parents would arrange and the bridegroom they chose for her. The ceremony was performed when she was four years old and she stayed with her parents until they thought she was old enough to go to her husband's house. When she was about eleven years of age, she was moved to his home and a new life began for her. Her mother-in-law received her kindly, and her husband, who was a grown man, was gentle and thoughtful to her, except when he was displeased and then she had what she called her deserts.

They were a family of four sons, and all their wives lived there in that one house of the Headman of the village.

Life was not exactly serene, but it was as normal as could be under the circumstances. The little wife was in great demand to do all the little odd jobs that befall the youngest: but she was still a child and she wanted to play. When she got the chance, she was off to where the cows go to drink, paddling with other children, until a loud stern voice recalled her, and she had to get back quickly to clean the "bartans" and be kept busy with the menial tasks left for the youngest wife! And that was her life all day and every day. There are no Sundays in the reckoning of a Hindu family: ever day is the same, except the special festivals, of which there are plenty in a year, and these are kept and enjoyed to the full. Some required a special pilgrimage to the temple or place of bathing, and processions of women in a blaze of richly-coloured saris walk through the fields in single file, singing their songs of the gods they worship as they go, and life is not drab for that day at least.

A Hindu festival is near now, as I write, and thousands will go off to Nepal, walking with weary feet over roadless miles of country until they get to the "Border Line," where they may cross and enter the closed land.

I have been in a multitude of fifty thousand, and watched the eager faces, and heard the excited voices as they neared what is called "The Gate."

Women too old to walk are carried in deep baskets on the backs of coolies. The rich are taken in "palanquins," i.e., a long box with sliding doors with four long poles that rest on the shoulders of the men carried, and thousands just trudge along the dusty way day after day until they reach their destination where they can see the great Mahadeo, which is Mount Everest. There they prostrate themselves and lie on their faces in worship, and offer their prayers with presents to the priests, "for," they say "any prayer offered before the Great Mahadeo is sure of an answer": and the hungry-hearted pour out their longings, and the thirsty souls hope to be satisfied. They give all they have, and having done all they can, they turn and set their faces back to the families they left in search of peace.

I have met them on the way and talked with them of their desires and what they have done to gain salvation. "Are you satisfied?" I asked a company of three Brahmin widows, and their faces lit up with eagerness. "Oh yes," they said, "we have seen the Great Mahadeo, we have worshiped there, we have walked many days' journey. See our feet, they are swollen, cut and bleeding, but we got there. Yes, we are satisfied that we have had a sight of the pure white Mahadeo, but—but—it is not enough," and the woman put her hand on her heart and with very wistful eyes looking into mine, as if her soul searched mine, she said: "It isn't enough for my heart. I did see with these eyes, but my heart—my heart is empty." She looked unutterably sad, and then I said to her: "Blessed are the pure in heart for they shall see God." I repeated the words and asked her if she knew how to be pure in heart. She talked fast of all she had done, all she had suffered, and of the burdens she had carried, "but, for my heart, it is not enough," she repeated. "Who can have a pure heart?" she asked, and then I suggested that we sit by the roadside and read from a Book I had that told us how we may have a heart that is pure and clean and the three Brahmin widows sat down close to me while I read: "The Blood of Jesus Christ, God's Son, cleanseth us from all sin. If we confess our sins, He is faithful and just to forgive us our sins and to cleanse us from all unrighteousness." And there I taught them to pray, "Create in me a clean heart, O God," and in the solemn hush of those wide open spaces they prayed their first prayer in the Name of Jesus.

We sat for a very long time, talking together of salvation and the Saviour, and there they learned His Name, and asked me to write it down on a bit paper that they might carry it with them wherever they went.

Then they went on their way, but they turned back again and again, for something in the Name had gripped them, and at last, I saw them in the distance going on their way to face life again, with the old things and the old ways, but what they heard that day, so new to them, will never grow old, for it is the Word of God, that is LIVING and powerful, and I know He watches over His word to perform it.

O wondrous Name, how can I tell it?
How make His love so real it lives?

O spirit of the Living God anoint me
To say the Name of Jesus that it lives.

Thousands travel on this way every year: I met them yesterday, the same anxious, eager crowd, pushing forward to the place they have heard of where peace is to be found. We call Nepal a closed land, but it is wide open to them. The gods of Nepal are their gods. They worship and they suffer and they long for salvation, and we are sent to tell them how they may find rest to their souls. Often I say to myself:

Christ the Son of God has sent me
To the midnight lands.
Mine the mighty ordination
Of the pierced hands.

A nd then I kneel in prayer to have my lips touched with the fire from His altar, that I may speak the name of Jesus with a glow that will make Him real and living to others.

Lola was a mother when she was just beginning her teens, but the joy of motherhood was shrouded by a cloud, for her first child was a girl, and the disappointment in the family was great: what good could a girl do? How could she carry on the ancestral spirit of the father? Only a boy could do that, and the father wanted a son. The mother-in-law wanted one too, so did everybody else. It was a calamity instead of a joy to have a girl for the firstborn, and sorrow filled her soul: all her happiness died, and she walked as one in a dream.

Why were the gods angry with her? She had done her best to serve her husband and the family she was married into. Why? why? why? she questioned, and then, one day, she heard songs that were new and strange to her, and she listened to the refrain. A band of women wearing white saris had come to their village to tell the people of a remedy for sin: they told of One Who had said and was still saying: "Come unto Me, all ye that are weary and heavy laden, and I will give you rest." She had never heard of Him before, and she listened with a mind that did not believe. It was something new, and wonderful to hear of One Who called the weary, and she was fascinated as she listened. The women sang on and then they separated, and after a while one of them came where she was squatting by the village pool, and they began to talk. Lola listened as one in a dream, and then she went into the house to her child and to think.

It was a strange and wonderful story, and that was the only time she ever heard it in her village.

Those women never came back again and the memory of what she heard dimmed almost to extinction as time went on, but not quite, for it all came back to her long after when she was far away from the early scenes and life was a real battle to her! Then she remembered the women and the news they had brought to her village, and she wondered where those women were and what they were doing and if anyone else knew the story they told. She was 16 years old and still no son had been given, and the mother-in-law began to be impatient and her temper was expressing in stinging words! What sort of a wife was she? What had she done that the gods refused to give her a son, and heir to carry on the family traditions? Who was going to appease the family gods? They were angry, else why no son? Then in the midst of all this turmoil, cholera came to their village. It was very mild at first, but the monsoon brought other evils and the whole village succumbed to its ravages. The waterways were clogged with weedy grasses and flowers that thrive in water: the rain poured in torrents, and the fields were flooded: houses made of mud melted and collapsed, grass huts disappeared from the soaking land, and the country became a swap of water rushing in great force towards the river held sacred by ever Hindu.

All that could be done was done to save, but many people lost their lives trying to save their bits of household goods. Still the rains continued, and cholera swept from village to village, carrying whole families in its grip, and very few recovered. Lola and her family were marooned in their house at the end of the village. An

Indian doctor could only get to them in a little boat cut out of a tree trunk, and he paddled himself across the great stretch of water to find a family unable to move.

The scourge had then in its grip, and the mother-in-law lay dead across the doorway. He stayed to help as long as he could, but when the night shadows fell across the face of the waters, all that remained of that family was a baby girl and two widows.

The wail of the bereaved fill the hot damp night. O the sorrows of India, so swiftly they come, so devastating they pass, and a crouching widow is left in misery. Without hope she sits; there is no relief. Her lord and master has gone, the gods have been displeased, who can appease them? Lola, with her double tragedy of a daughter instead of the expected son, and now a widow bereft of all she had, threw herself at the edge of the water in abandonment to grief. What had she to live for? Nothing! Hopeless an in poverty she must drag through an existence that is untellable. What could she do? Where could she go? Was there any such a sorrow as a Hindu widow's? No one to love, no one to care, despised and neglected by all her co-religionists, she, with her big disappointment of her unwelcomed child, now bereft of its father, must face the world and suffer together. She held her disappointment in her arms close to her heart and felt its warmth and sat there in misery. Her sister-in-law was with her, and they stayed in that house of death until someone came to take them away. Lola had her child, the other widow had nothing: her little son had died in her arms, and she held it there until it was taken from her.

Sorrow upon sorrow, grief that has no relief, they squatted in their misery, and both of them ill. "How could they live?" we asked, and yet they did, and when the waters had subsided and a way from the village appeared, they left the desolation and returned to their parents.

Lola said she was not welcomed, and she wouldn't stay. So she began her pilgrim life, joining with other widows as they went from temple to temple, walking long weary miles and traveling ticketless journeys to trains that carried passengers to holy cities, seeking, ever seeking, a peace that eluded her. She went to Prayag, to Ajodhya, and on to Benares, and there she stayed for some time and joined in the ever-moving crowds from temple to temple, never to miss an opportunity to bathe in the Sacred Ganges. From there she wandered to Calcutta, and was lost in the life of the women of the temples and for two years she served: and then, having heard of the city of widows, she began her pilgrimage again. Her baby girl was left with a friend in the temple, and being free of that burden she was eager to press on with other widows on her way, but she didn't get far, for sickness had her in its grip. She stopped at wayside temples and slept in the open, too ill to travel as others were doing, and she was left behind. She always met with kindness and the people in the villages shared their meagre food with her, but she reached a stage where she could go no further, and there, just there, was a hospital, known as a place of mercy. For two days she sat by the roadside, too frightened to go inside and too timid to ask for the help waiting for her there. But her agony drew the attention of passer-by, and it was reported to the doctor that a very sick woman was lying by the roadside, and soon strong arms lifted her up and carried her to a place of safety. She was too ill to notice anything: all she knew was that her body was broken, her honor gone, and she had no desire to live: but that made no difference to the doctors and the nurses. They saw her need and set out to meet it, and Lola was in that hospital for a very long time.

When she left, it was to go to a place where she would be received and welcomed, for she wanted to see Him Who had said: "Come unto Me all ye that labour and are heavy laden, and I will give you rest," and that is how she came to us.

THE TIDE IS SURE TO WIN

ALL THE STORMS *that gather round me,*
    Every hurricane's cold blast,
    Every storm-tossed billow blowing,
Through my being, swift and fast;
Take me onward if I let them,
Onward, onward to my goal,
For the winds of God now blowing,
Sent by Him to cleanse my soul.
They will blow the refuse from me,
Making sweet the air within,
Cleansing, purifying wholly,
From the stain and power of sin,
Waves of loss roll o'er and o'er me,
Crying "failure," loud and long,
All defeated they would leave me,
But I hear a distant song.
"Hallelujah, Hallelujah,
Jesus saves from every sin."
Waves of doubt may roll around me,
But there's calm and peace within,

For I've heard the song of triumph,
Through the crashing, roaring din,
Storms and billows overwhelm me
But the tide is sure to win.
God is in it, God is in it,
All through life's tempestuous sea,
On the tidal waves now running,
He will safely carry me.
Oh the glory there is in it,
For I know He loves me so,
Victory, victory, is my watchword,
Since I heard Him say--"Let go."

🦋 10 🦋

THE AWAKENING

THE AWAKENING
"YOU KNOW, you can't expect to see miracles nowadays, they are not done, they are not needed."

The speaker was a fine-looking person who seemed to know what he was talking about. It had no reference to anything I was doing. He was talking about the conditions in the world. "And," he continued, "you see, we are far too matter-of-fact, and too materialistic! Even in religion they are taboo, for no one accepts the miracles as a fact in life nowadays!"

I looked in amazement at the confident speaker.

"And suppose I say that I have seen miracles myself," I answered. "I could show you some if you came with me."

He looked at me from head to foot, staring as if he had seen a curio, and I repeated; "I could show you the results of a miracle: nay, of many miracles if you will come with me."

But he held his ground, muttering under his breath: "You must be living in the Middle Ages and deluding yourself." And I stood there and thought of what had just happened in the compound where I live, while I listened to him. He was quite sincere, he meant all he said, but he had missed something as he passed through life, and only a miracle could open his eyes that he might see: for except a man be born again, he cannot see. The Saviour said so Himself, and He understood perfectly: no amount of searching reveals the mystery of the kingdom, no amount of wealth will buy an entrance to that place of heart rest. Our Lord has "left us with a clear explanation of how to see and to know in those explicit words, Ye must be born again," and there is only disappointment to those who try to see and know and even to be until that transaction has been made. Oh, I am so glad and thankful that this same Jesus was so direct and that He spoke plainly just for love, because He wanted everybody to know the way, and that no one could possibly miss the beginning.

I went home to the family and sat back to think. Why do people not believe in miracles? I looked across the compound and I saw women walking about busy with the demands of a household, and I know that each of those I am looking at now have had that greatest of all miracles performed in them. They were Hindu or Moslem. Now they are followers of the Meek and Lowly Jesus. They are born again. How did this happen? The story of one is this, and it is not founded on fact, it is fact. A few years ago a young widow came to see a friend who lived here. She saw for herself those that had been saved, she asked many questions, and then she asked to stay, and we accepted her in the name of the Lord. Her child went into the class room and began to learn to read and write in his own language, but the widow scorned the idea for herself--how could she learn? she asked. She was only a woman and a widow at that: and a strange smile hovered over her face. So we left her alone to think things over. "I have never seen a woman read," she said. "Books are for boys and men," and she began to help cook the food for the family, and talked very hard while she did it. "This is a strange place," she remarked. "Girls learning to read and write. What is the good of it all? They are not going to be baboos (i.e., clerks)." We smiled with her, telling her that wonderful things are happening nowadays and Indian women are not only able to read and write--

they go to College, like men, and some of them even become doctors.

She opened her eyes wide in astonishment. "I've never seen one," she remarked. There are none in the place where I come from." And I thought of the villages where we go regularly, and the villages further off that can only be visited in the cold weather. Thousands live there, but there is no doctor!

She settled with us and learned to knit and it was a very serious business for her: stitches were dropped and were picked up, the width increased and decreased, and the length grew into an amazing dishcloth which she held up to me in triumph. She had tasted the joy of creating—where would it lead her?

She continued in the knitting class until she could knit a vest, and then something stirred within her. What if she should learn to read? Another like her who had been with us longer, had learned! She could read the book of the songs they sang, she had watched her sing with others, and she opened a book when someone read at prayers. She was changing, the eyes of her understanding were opening, and one day I saw her in school, her head bent low over a little book, her body swaying in rhythm, as she repeated the characters aloud; it was her first Primer!

How I wish you could have seen her. If knitting was important, all her world moved with her change of mind, and she fought with her memory that refused to work. What she learned today slipped away, and every day she began again. Week after week, she was hard at it, always in the first page of the Hindu Primer!

What could be done? What was the matter? Why could she not remember her lesson from day to day? She could remember other things. I puzzled about this and tried various ways of helping her remember those lines she went over so often every morning, but she never got beyond the first page until something happened. For two years she went into the class every day. The teacher gave a compassionate smile and said, "She will never learn to read: what is the good of her coming into school? She has no brains." and I wondered what the block was. She came to us with scar on her soul. She had sinned and kept her secret; never once had she acknowledged it, and as I watched and waited and prayed, I wondered how long she would be able to go on; "Oh, if only the Holy Spirit would convict her" I said within myself.

"I wonder what hinders that woman from getting on. She never moves forward," Elsie remarked, and I answered "I think her soul is paralyzed: we must get to prayer and pray her through. She has been with us over two years, she is not too old to learn to read, and there is no response to spiritual things."

Again I asked the Lord to show me how to help her. It came very quietly and naturally in the daily contact.

We were together on the back verandah: she was sorting out some things for the children and I joined her. After a time, I stopped and looked into her face, questioning her of something in the past. She looked vacant for a bit, but I saw her fingers twitch and her lips tightly close. I was relying on the Holy Spirit doing His work and I kept still in the Lord.

"When He is come," I said to myself. "He will convict of sin," and there I stood and closed my eyes and prayed to be so filled with the Holy Spirit that He could and would show her what was hindering her. She was in no hurry to move and I stayed with her. After a time, I said to her: "If it would help you to tell me, I will wait, but you must tell God. There is something you must put straight or you will never get on."

And then I saw a splash, and tears were raining down her face, so I drew her inside my room and we knelt down together.

"There was no hurry, time was no object. Her sin had come to the top: it was now or never for her decision--and I waited. If you have ever knelt with a sinsick soul you will understand.

I cried unto God for her, "Lord, save her *now*," I said. "Save her or she will perish," and suddenly her cry rent the air. She never thought to be found out, but He had found her, and she was humbled in the dust.

"I did it, I did it," she cried. "I did it, I did it," she repeated and the convicting power of the Holy Spirit held her until she had confessed it all. And then I repeated the words from the Book: "If we confess our sins, He is faithful and just to forgive us our sins and to cleanse us from all unrighteousness. The blood of Jesus Christ, God's Son, cleanseth us from *all* sin--cleanseth us from all sin, *cleanseth us* from all sin"--it was finished.

The change in her was tremendous. It was as if something had burst within her, and she was made free. I watched with solemn awe as I perceived how God was leading her in the paths of right-eousness. She began to make the crooked things straight, she cleared her own path, and then she decided to have another try with her Primer.

The teacher greeted her with the same pitying expression but there was a new light on her face and a great hope within her. She had seen the advantage of reading and a great longing was born within her that she might so learn that she could read the Word of God for herself.

Her first new day was spent as usual, but she was awakened, and a great determination mastered her. She was going to read, and when school time was over and her work was done, she took down her one and only book to find that she really did remember what she had tried to learn in the morning. It was amazing to her, but it was true, and day by day after that time she found the impossible made possible. There was nothing superficial about her, she had faced the fact of sin and felt its devastating work, and now that she was saved she set out to prove it.

From the Primer she was soon reading her first book of words; somehow or other, when that something broke inside her, a freedom she had never known became hers. She walked about the compound with dignity and purpose. Old things were passed away: she was a new person. Her childishness disappeared as she passed from one class to another. We were forgetting the things that are behind and reaching forward to the things that are before. Some-thing about her drew all our hearts, she was so gentle and unas-suming, and we watched and wondered what God would do with her.

Her little boy, grown big, was sent away to school to be with other boys, and she talked of what he would do when he became a man. The joy of a mother is unlike anything else. Something about him inspired her to rise. She asked to learn many things, including caring for the sick, caring for a little family, doing all she could to help others. She made happiness wherever she was working, and life opened out possibilities she had never dreamed of.

I can see her now, going out with others to give her witness at one of the dispensaries, coming back to tell others what she had done, surprised at her own achievements, increasing in knowledge and the fear of the Lord.

How glad I am that we had the privilege of having her here, and that God gave to us the unspeakable joy of seeing the soul's awakening.

BEHOLD, HE COMETH!

SO NEAR—SO near His coming,
    He may come any day,
    These war clouds sent to herald
The Bridegroom in his way,
Are but His chariots speeding
Through time, for close at hand
Is Christ—the Coming Saviour,
Sent from Immanuel's Land.
Jesus the Lord of Glory,
Will soon be back again,
Jesus the King of Glory,
Is coming back to reign .
We love—love His appearing,
Watch for Him every day,
These war clouds tell us plain
Jesus is on His way.

❧ 12 ❧

UP TO DATE

GOD MOVES IN A MYSTERIOUS WAY, His wonders to perform,
      He plants His footsteps in the sea, and rides upon the storm.

It was the year 1944, the beginning of the first month, and I sat down to collect my thoughts and to ponder over the mysterious way He had led us. The dark valley had been passed through: He was with us there and had spoken to our hearts, and we accepted His word to dig ditches and to make wells, and now we wait and watch for the harvest; surely there will be one, for He said, "The valleys shall be full of corn!" and we know that He means exactly what He says. We have proved also that

There is no gain but by a loss,
You cannot save but by a cross.
The corn of wheat to multiply
Must fall into the ground and die.

The beginning of the past year would have been hopeless for us had He not spoken the word, "Be of good cheer, It is I, be not afraid," and morning by morning we awoke to a new day that held the opportunity to trust and not be afraid.

The rapid changes all around gave no time for superficial thinking; we were faced with the impossible, and having done all we could, we had to stand and God worked the miracle. All through that fourth year of war there were new discoveries, some painful and some that came leaping to us like joy let loose. We paused to consider, and that always sent us to our knees. We wonder how others can live through these days without Him. He is so needed, and so wonderfully precious to them that believe, and He makes all the difference in the world to the situation as it is, wherever we are, whatever we are doing.

I took my Bible up again and read Mark 6:35-54. Why are we always quoting those words? How is it that the miracle of feeding five thousand people with five loaves and two small fishes is the definite challenge to us nowadays? Somehow or other it always raises a desire to see the thing done, and always compels to action with the statement: "If He could do that, He could do this." The situation we are in changes its aspect: we see Him, and He is "the same yesterday and today and forever." So why not tell Him everything and see what He will do? Thus we stopped everything—yes, stopped is the word—and we gathered together to face things as they were, and then He spoke: "Believest thou, that I am able to do this?" Our hearts cried a joyous "yes" for we knew in Whom we had believed.

War news was depressing--the enemy was coming nearer. The place which was home to nearly two hundred of us might be needed for something else. We were more than warned, and we faced what to us was an impossible situation. Our cry went up and God came down, and He delivered us from all our fears. He is the God of the widow, He is the Father of the fatherless. All we had had been put into His hands. He is able to keep our family, that which we have committed unto Him, and we watched to see how He would do it.

We remembered how He gave us this place, and talked of the

miracles He had performed for us year after year, and how He had come to us and made us His very own *and told us so.*

We looked at the children, and the women, and then we discussed the boys--fifty of these still needed to be fed and clothed and trained to earn their own living. Letters from their school told of the difficulty of food supply: and everyone seemed to need clothing. The tiny people ran about in skimpy garments they had grown out of, the girls drew their saris round them to hid wear and tear, and everything and everybody seemed to be in need of something. I sat before the Lord to talk to Him about it. I read His promise again, and then I turned to the leaves to Mark 6 and began to read again how our Blessed Lord fed those five thousand people with five loaves and two small fishes. Then I looked up: He was there, and I told Him of the need of clothes for the children, and I heard Him say: "How many have you? Go and see," and I got up and went into the room where most of the clothing is kept.

I unlocked a box and began to count, and I spoke to Him as if I could see Him. "Twenty-seven of these," I said, 'fourteen of these," and I turned to another box and, after counting, told Him the number. Then I opened every box and cupboard and displayed the contents. But he had asked me "How many?" and so I counted all there was and He never left me. I knew He had asked me an intelligent question and He expected and intelligent answer; so I wrote it all down and a solemn awe came over me.

"Why so very particular about the clothing of these children?" I am asked sometimes. I remembered a day when He said to me, "I was naked and ye clothed Me," and I began to think, clothes and clothing, did they matter to Him? And He answered: "Inasmuch as ye did it unto one of the least of these My children, ye did it unto Me"; and clothing from that hour had a holy meaning.

I picked up a little colourful kurta and looked at the careful stitching. I looked at the buttonhole so beautifully made, and thought of a young girl in a far-away village in England who expressed her love to Him in the garment she had made for a little child in India whom she had never seen. I looked at the pile of "pinnies" made of soft blue material that never fades in the sun and I thought of love for Him expressed in a class of girls, called Crusaders, who live in a city in the Midlands. I held up some jerseys from a box near--so beautifully made, they took hours to knit--and they came from a village in Norfolk. They had just arrived. I held them up to Him, but no one would be more surprised than they to hear Him say: "Inasmuch as ye did it unto one of the least of these, ye did it unto *Me*." Their love is so lavishly poured out: their time so unstintingly given, and the quality of their work makes one wonder, sometimes, if these children here will ever understand the love that clothes them. Personally I firmly believe that what is put into a gift somehow or other reaches the soul of the received, and that is the richness of the clothing three women and children wear. I stood there with every box open and every cupboard shelf showing what was there and then I said: "Dear Lord Jesus, I have all these but what are they among so many?" and there I knelt while His peace flooded my soul. I knew I was understood, and came out to tell Bertha. She too had been counting the things she had, and the things she needed for the education of the family, and we stood there in His presence. He seemed to fill the bungalow, and my heart sang its song of love to him Who had given to us such an unrivaled opportunity to see what he could do. It is wonderful to be consciously in His Holy Presence all the day long. Every hour was hallowed.

Even while we stood there the postman arrived with a parcel. It had come a perilous journey through danger zones and mine-infested seas: ships were torpedoed and damaged, and many were sunk, but a parcel of little garments for His lambs in the fold arrived intact. We opened it with awe but we said very little: we were too solemnized by the realization of the difficulties of the way. He makes a way in the sea, and nothing is a difficulty to Him. The parcel contained new "pinnies" and "pyjies" for twenty-four little ones, and the earnest of more to follow--all this when nothing can be bought without a coupon! What can we say to such love and sacrificial giving? Those garments were made by a group of people in a lovely mission hall right in the heart of the county, where they constantly heard the planes overhead and sometimes heard the bombs dropping and the reality of war was their continually. They were not thinking of themselves and their dangers, they were thinking of little children far, far away, and because they loved the Giver of Salvation, they expressed it in deeds that again sent us to our knees in worship and adoration.

They were lovely little garments, beautifully made to a pattern ours always wear, sacred garments that tell us we are loved and not forgotten, and when we put them on our little people we put our arms around them to help them feel the love that gave them and the love that made them. Little hands stoke them and look admiringly at the colours, and they feel loved. Could anything be better for them? Could anything be more lovely? And what is one of the ways they learn to sing with assurance:

Jesus loves me, this I know,
For the Bible tells me so,
Little ones to Him belong,
They are weak, but He is strong.
Yes—Jesus loves me

☙ 13 ❧

HIS PRESENCE—ALL DAY

AT MORNING TIME He came to me,
    And took my hand in His,
    He washed me in His precious blood,
And filled my heart with bliss,
He set me out along the road,
Himself to be my Guide,
And oh! The joy as through the day
I felt Him at my side.
When noon drew near, my hand He clasped,
More firmly than before,
He closer came, I leaned on him,
More than in days of yore.
And as I leaned, He whispered low,
"My own--keep at my side,"
As I obeyed I found that He
My heart had satisfied.

The dawn has passed and noonday too,
　　But He is more to me,
　　Than all my dreams in bygone hours,
I fancied He could be.
The evening hour is on the wane,
But I can have no fear,
When darkness comes I feel His hand,
I know He is quite near.

My birthdays come and come again,
　　And I His leadings trace,
　　But oh! what rapture will it be,
When I shall see His face.
The sudden rending of the sky,
The billowing clouds divide;
A swift glad meeting with His own,
The Bridegroom and the Bride.

✿ 14 ✿

IT IS A MIRACLE

I WAS RIVETED—"THEY considered not the miracles" (see Mark 6:52). They had forgotten, and so had we until we began to count our blessings and the pile heaped up before us. "The Lord hath done great things for us," we said to each other: "we will rejoice and be glad," and I began to talk of the miracles He had wrought for us. How could we define them in these days when people say the days of miracles are over? Are they? Listen!

It had happened--the miracle!--we saw the gleam in the eyes of our women when their souls were awakened. We watched the Light dispel the darkness, and looked for the Daystar to arise in their hearts, and He came in--quiet power and lifted them one by one out of the depths of the impossible into a life that freed them from the past. Old things passed away, behold, all things had become new, and they knew it. Their walk declared it. They no longer liked to hide behind a pillar when we crossed the compound. They came out into the light and smiled the joy they felt, and their movements began to declare their freedom. They know the meaning of those words: "When He, the Son, shall make you free, ye shall be free indeed." They walk now with the freedom of the free, and they stand before you erect and sure of their position. They are found in Christ, fellow-heirs with the saints in Light, our children, our comrades, now our fellow-workers, sharers together of the grace of life, and yet, without that miracle they would never have been what they are today. I look back, and I remember, and those with me tell of things happening, and, lest we forget, I am writing it down for His glory, that you too may know what He has done and is doing here.

He has given to us the message of reconciliation to pass on to these people, that they may see and understand that this salvation is for them. They believe it, receive it, and enter into things unseen, but revealed to those who diligently seek Him.

I think of a little trembling, discontented widow with a child in her arms, brought over a thousand miles to a place of safety. She had suffered the penalty of widowhood when not much more than a girl and had been turned adrift, unwanted, uncared for, despised, neglected, with no safe place to dwell in, no anchorage for her frailty: she was adrift when Jesus found her and brought her to a hospital where she could get what she needed for her body, and there she met one of His sent ones who lived looking for the lost, and she told her of the Saviour.

Our little widow did not believe that anyone cared for her. Hadn't she been battered and pushed about among the despised and rejected?

All her belief centered round the fact that she was a little Hindu widow, therefore cursed of the gods. How could anyone care for her? She was sure that no one loved her, except, yes, except the little bit of humanity held close to her breast, for that was all she had, and the only fight she had in her was for her child.

They fed her in the hospital and helped to free her from the aches and pains in her body, and as strength came, she began to take notice. There was a nurse there, who was a widow like herself, and yet, she was different: what had made the change? Why did people respect her? Ask for her help? Obey her injunctions? Why? She asked herself, and watched, and one day the nurse bent over her and said: "I know Some One Who can help you, Who will save you. I will ask Sister to send you to a place where you will find Him: she knows all about it." But the little widow didn't believe a word of it. She only thought it was another trap to hold her down, and her spirit rose in defiance. No, she was not going to any other place, she was going to stay in the hospital where she felt safe and was sure of help and, the wonder of wonders, where she was not despised, and she stayed on until they could keep her no longer and she had to choose.

Where was she to go?

She walked about the wards trying to get conversation with the other widow who was busy nursing, and bit by bit, she told her about Jesus the Mighty to save. "He has saved me, and He will save you," she said, "if you are willing." Then, there was the word with the Sister, His sent one, and the little widow asked for a place of safety, and early one morning she arrived here.

Little frightened Hindu widow, her attraction was her dire need, and yet, she had no intention of staying. She had come merely to see: her body was broken, her soul in darkness, but her child held tightly to her; Thus we took her in. What could we do with such a frail little woman? She looked like a wisp that the wind would blow away. I am looking back and thinking, remembering the first weeks and days when all seemed wrong with her and she came like a waft of wind saying, "I am not going to stay here, I don't like the place," and I answered, "The prayer bell has just gone; come, let us go into the House of God." As always, the same thing happened: the little widow was calmed in His presence and came out to begin the day trying to learn to read, so that some day she could read the word of God for herself. But it was a slow process for her mind was not given that way; her thoughts were on her child. He was a boy and an object of worship, and it was a full-time job. All her time, every minute of it, was given to doing something for and to her one and only treasure. She had food and clothes for both of them. She had shelter. Why turn aside to learn to read?

No, no, for the present she was here, but no amount of talk brings conviction--only the Holy Spirit can convict of sin and the need for conversion, and we know that He comes to live in hearts and lives opened wide for Him, and we know also that if He dwells in us, He will do his own work: it is not preaching that does the work, it is making it possible for the Holy Spirit to convict and convince of sin by being filled ourselves and letting Him have all there is of us so that He can do the work He came to do in those He brings to us.

"What do you think?" said Bertha one morning. "The little seven-year-olds are asking to have gardens and I said that I would speak to you about it." It means a little plot about three feet wide and six feet long, marked out and dug for each child, and I thought it out with the remark: "Why shouldn't they have their own gardens?" and at once gave the order for the positions to be measured out and marked.

So Bertha went back to the class and said: "We will give the land, but we have no seeds or plants for you." They looked at each other, and then one ventured: "We will ask God our Father and He will give them to us," and she left them at that. On thinking it over, she returned to say that they would all go to her room for a prayer meeting at 5 o' clock. They smiled their assurance and continued their lessons. They all have a break in the middle of the morning, and as Bertha crossed the compound to her dismay she saw ten little girls lying on their faces on the class room floor. Stepping up to see the reason why, she heard little voices praying: "O God our Father, we want to make a garden for Thee and we have no plants, and we have no seeds." One after another prayed, unconscious of any listener but God. Standing near them was our little Hindu widow, watching, wondering what it was all about. Bertha whispered to her, and led her away to explain that they wanted to make a garden. Mamaji had given the ground, but they had no seeds or plants to grow there, so they were asking God for them.

"And will they get them?" asked the widow. "I am sure they will," Bertha replied. The little widow was intrigued.

At 5 p.m. the children came up for their prayer meeting, but they were quick to say that they had already prayed for plants and seeds. "Now we shall pray for something else," they announced, and that was that--they didn't believe in much repetition! So Bertha started off with Thanksgiving.

Next morning a gardener from one of the houses in the station arrived with a basket full of seedlings. "I wonder if you can use these," the lady wrote, "we have too many." She did not know that our children had asked God to send them, but He had sent them through her and we told her so, and she began to take an interest in prayer and the answers.

The joy in the compound was hilarious: the little people were so excited that their fingers trembled as they prepared the holes for the seedlings to plant them there themselves.

"*Our gardens,*" I heard them say. "God our Father sent the plants: we will have beautiful gardens;" and they walked around looking at others and their plots, and then back to their own first bit of land. How they love to see things grow! It is joy unspeakable to them, and I began to wonder--what next? When the little widow passed, she stood for a moment and turned to look back on ten little happy girls bending double over their gardens. "They prayed," she said to me. 'They were like this," suiting the action to the words. "Why does God give them what they ask? She inquired. "God is love," I answered. "He loves to give." She, poor thing, only knew that her god had to be appeased: there was always something to be done, something to be given up for him. The very fact that she was a widow was a proof of his displeasure: so her eyes opened wide in astonishment when I explained the love of God which passeth knowledge, and even as I talked with her, the wonder of our commission almost overwhelmed me. Sent to open the eyes of the blind, sent to set the captives free, sent with a message of reconciliation. God was in Christ, He came to save. Wonderful, wonderful, to be an ambassador for God, it is such a high and holy calling, how can we ever be worthy of it? How can we make others know how much He cares? Yes, "God is love." and we are watching to see how He will win her.

The gardens flourished and were gay and flowers in good time, and sometimes little hands clasped a bunch held out to me, sacred flowers given by God, and the radiant possessors danced with joy over their buckets of water.

The first thing the children learn about gardening is how to water it. When they have learned that, they begin to dig, then they prepare the land, then they sow the seeds, and it is a revelation of character how these children care: and having first learned to water, they understand how precious it is to the young plants entrusted to their care.

I look across from where I am writing and I see odds and ends of the family bending over their gardens, and it is a blaze of glory.

I walked across to the cottages the other day to where the converts live, and I saw a fine mixture in great profusion --onions and phlox, one tomato plant jammed with nasturtiums, and two dahlias and a rose tree, spots of mint and parsley, and there was one canna and some climbing pink antigonon in a patch of pepper, and a trail of morning glory ended the scene--but oh, what happiness it all gave: it is all their own, and that is bliss indeed.

The little widow pointed out everything to me: she knew all about things growing, and, pausing over the patch of onions and some pepper plants, she gave an affectionate glance, saying: "I planted these." Then she began to tell me again about the children she had seen and heard praying for seeds and plants, and she had talked with Bua about it. "How did they learn to pray?" she asked, and Bua's reply was; "Why don't you ask them?" So bit by bit she was learning the truth that God hears and answers prayer, and whatsoever we ask the Father in the Name of Jesus, we shall have. But Bua had said: "If you want to pray you must begin by asking God for a new heart, then He will put his Holy Spirit within you, and you will know how to pray and what to ask for." And so she went from one to another, questioning, and thinking and wondering, and it was a little girl who first led her into the Secret Place.

The child was ill in Bethany: her bed was on the verandah. The widow was visiting her, and they must have had some talk about Jesus, for I saw her kneel by the sick-bed, with her head half hidden, and the patient sitting up with hands clasped, and thus they stayed for some time. I could see them from the open door and I closed my eyes to pray for them. There was much coming and going in the rooms for the sick, and I notice how often the Lord meets them there.

"Now Jesus loved Bethany." I turn to the sacred pages, and we set to work to prepare for Him, and over and over again He answers our cry and His blessing is a very real thing there.

The little widow opened her heart to the light, and her attitude to life changed. She felt around to find no one was against her, all wanted her to know Him and with all her heart she sought and found Him. The miracle happened, and it was "not by might, nor my power, but by My Spirit, saith the Lord," and her heart was at rest.

The End

Printed in Great Britain
by Amazon